TRUMP

THE BIG LIE

DR. ROGER ROSENBERG

TRUMP & THE BIG LIE

Table of Contents

The Big Lie

Speaking of lies and liars: it seems to me people are so fixated on Trump's ONE BIG LIE about the 2020 election that they are forgetting the extremely long chain of dubious claims he made over the last four years. Some of his statements were mind-boggling but his trips into the Land of Falsehood were even more inexplicable and sometimes repulsive.

This is not his first lie and it certainly won't be his last. People who don't want a liar in the White House found abundant reason to vote him out of office. Here are a few reminders . . . .

TRUMP'S "VIEWPOINT"

- I am smarter than everyone.
- I have perfect hair.
- I earned all my money; my dad never helped me with $200,000,000.
- My dad's family is Swedish, not German.
- I never stiffed anyone.
- I never spent the night in Russia.
- Mexico will pay for the wall.
- I made "a perfect call" to the president of Ukraine (I illegally threatened to withhold

- money from his country; that's what made the call so perfect!)
- My swearing-in ceremony had a much bigger crowd than my predecessor. Photographs were faked or touched up to make it appear the opposite was true.
- I am consistent, never flip-flop, and never contradict myself.
- I never have to walk back statements I made because they are so inane nobody, not even my supporters, can believe I said what I did.
- I never embellish, exaggerate, or con people with half-truths.
- I do not create preposterous falsehoods out of whole cloth.
- I never put my foot in my mouth.
- "I could stand in the middle of Fifth Avenue and shoot somebody and I wouldn't lose any voters." (no, really!)
- I was a fabulous college student with all kinds of academic awards.
- I dutifully read everything my advisers leave on my desk to read.
- American journalism is fake news.
- Alternative reality is a well-known acceptable theory.
- I would never ask or expect my subordinates to swear loyalty to me.
- I would never engage in nepotism for light or transient reasons.

- I was never impeached; that's the media's fake news.
- John McCain was no hero (if not for bone spurs I might have served: now *that's* heroic!)
- I am not prejudiced toward black people.
- I do not know why white supremacists support me: just lucky, I guess!
- I will release my taxes . . . any decade now.
- I will go to court and swear under oath James Comey does not understand why personal loyalty to the president is more important than loyalty to the Constitution.
- I never had sex with a porn star named Stormy Daniels.
- I never made her sign a non-disclosure form.
- I never authorized Michael Cohen to pay her $130,000 to keep her quiet nor did I tell Michael Cohen I would pay him back. If he says I did, that proves he doesn't know me! (Why Michael paid her that much money on my behalf, I don't know.)
- I don't know Karen McDougal, either.
- I don't know any of the women making accusations of inappropriate sexual abuse and behavior against me.
- I never made those lewd remarks on the "Access Hollywood tape" because I do not mistreat women or act aggressively toward them. All the women who say I do are making things up.

- Okay, maybe I made the comments but it was only "locker room" talk.
- The women accusing me of this stuff and trying to sue me are nasty.
- I never make insulting comments about people although it might seem that way to stupid people who can't handle my sense of humor which is terrific.
- I never pursued policies that were socially divisive.
- I never brought violence-prone malcontents and white supremacists crawling out of the woodwork by the busload to become my noisiest supporters.
- I don't know what Michael Cohen did because I barely know him and that means he's like less than nothing to me. He worked as my guy for a lot of years but we never really talked. Once he jumps off the Trump yacht he's on his own even if he starts to drown.
- I don't know who Rudy Giuliani is because I barely know him and that means he's like less than nothing to me (especially if he keeps screwing up!)
- I don't know who _____ is either (it pays to keep a blank form on hand!)
- The Corona Virus will go away by itself. Everything is great.
- Drink bleach if you want to be safe from the virus.

- My enemies call me a Narcissist because I am the smartest guy in the whole world.
- I eat healthy with a lot of 'burgers and Coke which is why I am not at all overweight.
- I was not sick when they rushed me to the hospital. The doctors didn't know what was wrong with me but it wasn't Covid-19 because I don't catch diseases regular people get.
- I don't cheat at golf. All my golf buddies who keep insisting otherwise are fibbers.
- I never ordered the police to clear the park simply to make room for a photo opportunity (okay, that's one thing I did do, ha ha!)
- I am not a sore loser. I REPEAT: I AM NOT A SORE LOSER!
- My inflammatory remarks on January 6th were meant to keep the crowd calm.
- I was as surprised as anyone when my supporters attacked the Capitol to prevent Congress from certifying the election in which I was defeated by seven million votes.
- I happen to know the election was much closer than that. In fact I'm sure I won by a landslide because everyone loves me.
- Who is stupid enough to believe that my four wonderful years in office could produce a majority wishing to vote me into retirement? That's not plausible because I am the greatest president who ever lived!
- I know what I'm doing.

- I'm not in any legal trouble.
- I'm not worried I might get dementia.
- I'm not worried I might already have dementia.
- I will be reinstated in August 2021, just you wait and see.
- I will be the first president in history to have both Narcissism and Dementia at one and the same time and that will make me the greatest president ever for my next three terms!
- I will become president for life! (just like my friend Putin!)

****

Trump's Warped Reality

The ex-president loved to lie about a number of things. You know, Trump's lineage is demonstrably Germanic yet he lied and insisted it was Swedish. It is an interesting trait, is it not, this zealous commitment to defending the most outlandish lie, no matter how preposterous? Most liars try to be clever and avoid being caught but some liars practice their craft "out in the open." They not only lie about themselves but they are even quicker to accuse others of being the deceitful ones, even when there is no evidence, which is invariably the case.

Trump accused Barack Obama of not being a U.S. citizen and challenged him to produce a birth certificate to prove otherwise. Clever tactic, is it not? If Obama ignores the request, Trump can claim he was afraid to face the accusation. Eventually Obama had to respond; in due time the "short form" birth certificate was produced. Could Trump admit that he was wrong and apologize? No, not him; another of Trump's curious traits is he never admits he was wrong, even after it has become apparent to everyone that he was. Instead, he changes direction and modifies his false accusation. Most Americans knew Obama was an American and the short-form birth certificate was sufficient *documentary proof*. Trump, however, was not done with his spurious allegation. He deflected growing criticism by insisting Obama was afraid to show, or did not have, the "long form" birth certificate that was once standard before the short form was adopted. Obama made the necessary arrangements to produce that birth certificate, too. It showed that Obama was born in Honolulu at Kapiolani Hospital on August 4, 1961. That made him a natural-born American citizen. Yet Trump kept hammering away at this false accusation...for what purpose? To end up having to concede the point in question?

No, he wouldn't have set himself up for failure that way if there wasn't something bigger in it for him. More likely, this particular false accusation was part of testing his followers, a way to probe the depth of their racist sentiments. He was sending up a "nuanced" trial balloon and measuring the intensity of the response. His false accusations against Obama certainly resonated with white supremacists; Trump came to realize he could count on them as a significant portion of his base. To that end of not offending white supremacists, Trump carefully avoids making any comments that affirm principles of equality and justice for America's minorities, African-Americans in particular. He nearly choked trying to find a way to criticize the pro-Nazi group that marched in Charlottesville, North Carolina, even after their actions led to the killing of an innocent peaceful protestor, Heather Hier by name.

For those who like to track backwards, Trump's racism was undoubtedly inherited from his father; Fred Trump engaged in illegal housing practices, like refusing to rent to black people: "The Justice Department sued Donald Trump, his father, Fred, and Trump Management in order to obtain a settlement in which Trump and his father would promise not to discriminate. The case eventually was settled two years later after Trump tried to countersue the Justice Department for $100 million for making false statements. Those allegations were dismissed by the court."[1]

Such skirt-the-law practices appeared to be the preferred *modus operandi* for Trump's father, an outlook on life passed on to his son; instead of "Honesty is the best policy" the maxim is rewritten more bluntly: "Dishonesty is not a bad thing if you can get away with it." Trump has become extremely smooth at telling his falsehoods, like he's had a lot of practice. Next, he enters a trance, a kind of hypnotic self-deception, wherein he pretends he is hearing the lie for the first time...as though it came from somebody else, *from an outside source*, even though he himself set

---

[1]**https://www.npr.org/2016/09/29/495955920/donald-trump-plagued-by-decades-old-housing-discrimination-case** retrieved 7/15/22.

11

the falsehood in motion. A cable news show is part of Trump's act, each claiming the falsehood must be credible merely because it was repeated back and forth between them!

One gets a good glimpse of the man's character if you look closely at this pattern of deception and exaggeration. One part of him invents falsehoods and pretends to believe them, expertly enough to convince others! That leads his most vociferous critics to doubt his intelligence and moral values; he appears "dumb" to them since he makes so many mistakes and blows so much smoke. However, another side of him appears quite shrewd and more than capable of knowing how to increase his personal fortune. He also promises to protect the wealth of the richest people in America. Since he is now counted among them, such a promise is eminently believable; billionaires stick together like birds of a feather.

That's the side that's very much alive, though sometimes hidden. As crazy as some of his utterances may seem, one must not underestimate Trump's ability for hard-headed realism and purposeful action when the mood strikes him. Is he a clown or a master manipulator? Sometimes it's hard to distinguish between the foolish foot-in-mouth Trump and the ambitious, wealth-seeking Trump. He muddies the waters when he offers sensationalized utterances that appear to come out of nowhere, which in turn will set off a media frenzy; this provides cover for his financial agenda and feeds into his ability to raise a great deal of cash from his base.

The real question to ask is: who is donating millions of dollars to his campaigns and where is the money going? Why is it so urgent that billionaires have another billionaire in the White House? Anyone can see at a glance that control over government spending produces innumerable opportunities to fleece the golden goose, especially if Trump and his backers have a practiced eye for weak spots in the financial system. Large sums of money can change hands and remain more or less untraceable. Whether from his cash-blessed family fortune or from the richest individuals and corporations in the country, Trump brings in the money. When the cash flow slows, get ready for his next outlandish statement and accusation.

He will work his base into a frenzy about something, anything, to fill up the coffers once more![2] His base is, after all, from a well-marked part of the political spectrum. It is not the usual liberal/conservative split we have seen from years gone by. Both sides would take jibes at the other yet remain committed to a democratic form of constitutional government, respecting the rights of free speech and conscience. They could disagree with each other while maintaining

---

[2] Ask yourself: when has the *loser* of an election ever raised as much money as Trump?

a civil tone and rational approach to the presentation of their best arguments and supporting facts. Now those days appear to be receding so rapidly into the past, it is as though they never existed.

The richest and most vocal Trump supporters have taken over the right-wing of the Republican Party and they are becoming less and less shy about making their presence and demands known. Certainly, there are still wealthy backers whose names are virtually unknown (who choose to remain deep in the shadows) but enough is understood of their monetary contributions to get a sense of what is happening. The link between great wealth and GOP leaders (supported by that wealth) is very obvious and becoming more and more exposed. When a person can afford to donate thousands or millions of dollars, the donor expects something in return. Trump dutifully promised a big tax break for the rich; that much was out in the open.

In terms of the so-called "culture wars," Trump is willing to take in cash from anyone, including the most racist elements in the country. He knows he can be as outspoken and unpredictable as he wishes and he won't ever lose *their* support; they like his agenda. For the wealthiest class, he stands for the kind of class-privilege stratification they adore. Whatever else can be said of his actions and beliefs, he continues to represent the richest of the rich. Not surprisingly, very wealthy individuals are donating *millions of dollars* to

Trump and his campaigns; his questionable antics do not appear to bother them in the least.

Here he follows a very sensible approach to life: represent the interests of the wealthy and watch the contributions flow. If he can strike just the right pose for conservative millionaires and billionaires, he can raise large sums of money; the wealthiest among his supporters will spend lavishly to maintain the Status Quo and their privileged positions within it. For them, every Democratic president since FDR represents something of a threatening nightmare; spending on social programs does little to increase their profits. Why else pour endless amounts of cash into Trump's campaign if not to urge him to try and reverse the liberal policies and programs of the Democratic Party?

In addition, generous giving from ordinary Republicans pumps up his war chest even more. His critics may see him as conceited but his followers seem to like his brand of charisma. His enemies find his arrogance repulsive, though one supposes that in his own eyes such arrogance is "justified" because he is smarter than everyone else. His grandiose Narcissism erroneously informs him, in an endless feedback loop, that he is *right about everything*. He is caught in a circular path in which his self-image is constantly exaggerating itself and which, in turn, touches off new bouts of unbridled boastfulness as well as inappropriate insults and condescending remarks. Is there anyone Trump would not cruelly insult if the moment or the mood compelled him to take a strong verbal jab? Occasionally he makes a half-hearted effort to control some of his worst excesses (impulses of narcissism) but how much stress that puts on his character is unclear.

One can almost feel the tension, the fight within him to "stick to the script" provided by advisers or to go loudly off-script and become Donald Trump again. He is already but a weakened shadow of his former self though more cautious critics surmise he may be "recovering" and biding his time. Still, there are incontrovertible facts that cannot be whittled down farther; he did not win a numerical majority in 2016 (only the-oddly tilted Electoral College saved him) and his popularity has not increased noticeably since then. He did, after all, lose the 2020 presidential election.[3] For an egoist like Trump, that's one hell of a bitter pill to have to swallow.

When he can hold the microphone in his hands and start "ad-libbing" like a comedian or a quirky politician, that was always a very special moment for Trump. Only then could he truly show how powerful he was. A narcissistic conceit like his craves "upping the ante" as they say in poker. He must try to outdo himself when

---

[3] He lost the popular vote by seven million votes; he also lost the Electoral College in 2020 *by the same margin* (306-232) that occurred four years before, which, in a historic twist of irony, he had called a "landslide" victory in 2016!

16

others least expect it; it is part of his psychological make-up to see just how big an outcry he can cause. There have been whispered rumors in the past about his temper and poor impulse control, his occasional confusion and unpredictability; there may be more to worry about if his condition deteriorates further, especially if he refuses to give up control over the party even though his declining mental health establishes itself so plainly that everyone can see it.

Poor judgment is one of the most prominent features of his narcissism; he has behaved so poorly and so unethically over the last few years that a surfeit of court cases involving alleged felonies are beginning to take shape all around him. What kind of values does an ex-president espouse that can land him in such hot water? At some point rank-and-file Republicans must begin to ask themselves (just in case) who should replace him if the need arises: should they go with another Trump loyalist to take his place or seize the moment and move away from Trumpism?

The crisis will begin to build in 2023 most likely; people will have a chance to see if Trump is still running the show or whether time and age are catching up with him. This would be somewhat comical were it not so tragic; the president's allies and cronies (aka "yes men") appear absolutely afraid to cross him to the slightest degree, as though he were the head of an organized crime family. What options remain for his advisers, no matter how much experience and expertise they may possess, when they are cowered into silence? What happens to the GOP if its most thoughtful advisers, wishing to offer him well-intended counsel, are made to fear risking his ire?

If a Republican "Big Boss" has grown so strong and powerful no one dares disagree with him, how does the GOP continue working out policy issues through the give-and-take of responsible representatives and experienced minds sharing their knowledge and thoughts? How does the GOP avoid becoming a party monopolized by a one-track narcissist? What a dangerous situation to create in the political life of America! Trump must know his behavior causes division and factionalism but he seems to relish this power to divide and antagonize. What happened to debate, to compromise, to toleration for multiple points of view? The obsequious Republican Party leaders either agree with Trump outright or are too afraid to confront him with their own viewpoint, which means the Party is in danger of becoming as one-dimensional as he is.

Why such a marked willingness to condone the actions of white supremacists? Why such a marked *unwillingness* on the part of the GOP to dissociate themselves from what once was called the "lunatic fringe" of the Far Right? Most GOP leaders failed to vigorously condemn the calamitous events of January 6th when a Trump-inspired crowd turned itself into an angry mob. They stormed the Capitol Building that houses the seat of American democracy, an attack which endangered the lives of brave police officers, elected congressmen and their hard-working staffers.

The historic GOP, the party (*nulli secundus*) for the last fifty years or more that always boasted the loudest that it was the party of law and order, now remains mum and tapes its own mouth shut while dozens of violent crimes are being committed in the capital; not merely ordinary crimes but an actual *insurrection* against a lawful proper election took place right before their eyes! Many of the GOP leaders choose to keep quiet or condone the riot, apparently; for some unfathomable reason, the party remains eager not to lose the support of those crazy violent insurrectionists. These rioters now join white supremacists as another significant section of Trump's base. Racists and Rioters! Sounds like a possible slogan for Trump's campaign for the 2024 election.

Trump remains a cash cow that can be milked; he keeps rivers of money flowing round while navigating the waters to see how far the Republican Party can go to the right in identifying with white supremacists, the better to antagonize and oppose moderate Democrats. Extremism on the Right is intended to make the political center appear farther away and subject to distortion and smear. Trump is, after all, the "charismatic" cultural icon of the Far Right. Extremist elements have been giving him their sincerest support from the very start. This relationship between the right-wing of the Republican Party and *even more extreme elements* seems to be solidifying itself and perhaps growing stronger. The current crop of timid GOP leaders appear all too willing to stick by him, or at least until something so unmistakably lethal arises in the body politic that he finally proves himself more of a liability than an asset.

Most of them will try to stick with him but if his bizarre behavior and reckless actions grow unabated, making election defeat more likely, the party will sooner or later have to reevaluate its options: stick with Trump despite the disastrous long-term effect he could have on the party, or support someone else? Sticking with Trump could end in electoral disaster but it must seem like the easier route for McConnell and McCarthy; there are precious few men of conscience among the Republicans willing to step forward and put constitutional principles ahead of Trump. Just such mistakes in judgment have dogged short-sighted leaders since time immemorial. They think they have found a short-term approach to winning an election and cannot see the political catastrophes that follow everywhere in Trump's wake.

They believe their logic makes sense: stick with a candidate already *twice impeached* and who *twice* lost the popular vote...and add to that the considerable damage done to his reputation *after* January 6 when millions of Americans awoke to the fact, in disbelief, that Trump attempted to negate the results of a free and fair election! He forcibly attempted a coup to try and remain in office, in other words. That would be called treason anywhere else; it is the ultimate dishonorable act of a self-centered autocrat and would-be usurper trying to seize power that does not belong to him but to the American people, who elected Joe Biden. He should have shaken President Biden's hand and wished him well. It's a simple act of courtesy and dignity but something Trump *refused to do*.

Nor should we forget the multiple lawsuits and prosecutions underway which could involve him in civil and criminal litigation for months and years to come. Perhaps his next announcement will be: if he is convicted of financial crimes or other offenses related to top-secret document possession, election-interference and insurrection, his followers should not worry about him for once he is president he will make it a priority to pardon himself! Can one imagine America ever reaching such a low point in the deterioration of its legal-ethical system that the nation would tolerate a convicted criminal *pardoning himself?*

If we begin that descent into national madness, that descent into hell, I personally would prefer to see a bona fide head of organized crime run the country. At least they know how to handle their ill-gotten gains more quietly and efficiently than Trump and his cronies ever did. The winds of Trump's make-believe world may swirl around him but he is not immune to the stronger winds of social change; his personality may grow more unstable and his actions more unpredictable once he sees cracks opening up among his followers and defections start to multiply, to say nothing of social changes in the wider political world that he cannot stop.

Over the last few years, there has been a strengthening of massive organized opposition to him and his policies. He serves as a magnetic galvanizing force for millions of democratic-minded Americans throughout the country; the election of 2020 proved it. His unpresidential behavior helped fuel the forces that coalesced to fight him tooth and nail. His arrogance, his temper, and his refusal to admit defeat will serve as a constant reminder to all Americans that he remains a very grave threat to the most cherished principles of our constitutional democracy.

The American people must be prepared to push back against his lies no matter how preposterous they are; they must push back against his attempts at character assassination and his willingness to spend gobs of money to denigrate others, fabricate excuses, and invent a fictitious "alternate reality" in order to hide his many inadequacies and brazen falsehoods. Do we really want a pathological liar as president? That is the question every American must answer!

****

Trump The Notorious Liar (2021)

I recall some time back a reporter on television had the audacity to mention Trump and Hitler in the same sentence. Another journalist took exception, believing that such a comparison was out of bounds. Perhaps it was but in the years since we learned the two leaders do have something in common: both men proved themselves inordinately fond of practicing the Big Lie technique. It appears that nearly everything they said was full of half-truths at best or was scandalously untrue at worst. Hitler lied regularly as leader of the Nazi Party and Trump does much the same as head of the Republican Party.

Of course, there are significant differences between world-conquest fascism in Germany in the 1930's and the embryonic state of authoritarianism happening here. Germany had precious little experience with democracy; the first few years of the Weimar Republic in the 1920's cannot be compared to the two-and-a-half centuries of the American Republic. Despite dark chapters of exploitation and oppression in our national history, generations of Americans have lived freely under well-established democratic institutions and traditions; no puff of wind can blow these principles away so long as the people themselves retain the original fighting spirit of what it means to be a free-born American.

Each generation must rise to the occasion to defend their nation from all enemies, foreign and home-grown.

These enemies now include domestic terrorists and, by political kinship, their associates in the Far Right of the Republican Party, a group which appears of late intent on warping American democracy into an unrecognizable form. Yet, as dangerous as these reactionaries are, they are not cut from the same cloth as the violent Nazi thugs who took power in Germany. Look at that nation's history: Kaiser Wilhelm, autocrat supreme, sat on the throne until 1918. By comparison, the U.S. was already on its twenty-eighth president, Woodrow Wilson (1913-1921). Germany itself only became a nation in 1871, joining together all the small principalities and fiefdoms under Otto von Bismarck's iron rule. Finally, at the end of World War I, the Kaiser abdicated; the Weimar Republic, born in the massive destruction of that war, was saddled with an enormous debt. Runaway inflation was soon exacerbated by the worldwide economic crash of 1929 on Wall Street and spread around the globe.

Under such near impossible conditions, the Weimar statesmen were expected to keep their nation on a democratic path but they were ill-prepared for the rise of Hitler, his propaganda and the violence of his storm-troopers. During the 1920's in the United States, Warren Harding, Calvin Coolidge, and Herbert Hoover became the twenty-ninth, thirtieth, and thirty-first presidents of the country, respectively. Thus, by the end of the decade the U.S. had already experienced thirty different presidents, dating back to Washington, Adams, and Jefferson, with each new president taking office through a peaceful transition of power. By the time of Harding, Coolidge, and Hoover the country had more than one hundred and thirty years of democratic experience behind it, and that was nearly a century ago.

The U.S. and Germany have distinct histories and while it is proper to note the occasional similarities in social development, it is just as crucial to recognize the differences. Our nation can be judged by its industrial capacity and technological innovations as well as by the political and social progress it has made from 1776 to the present. The Weimar Republic would have just fifteen years in power (1918-1933) before it fell to the Nazi Party. It was known as a constitutional federal republic, the first in Germany's history, but lacked institutional strength and stability. By contrast, the United States has held presidential elections and a peaceful transfer of power every four years since George Washington was elected in 1788-89. Not everyone could vote but among those citizens who could, the American presidents were democratically elected and the results accepted by all.

Hitler, on the other hand, soon turned to street terror to help secure his rise to power. He found a convenient scapegoat, the Jews, to serve as a rallying point for the brutality of his Brown Shirt terrorists. He built upon a long tradition of anti-Semitism in Europe and whipped it up into an irrational fury. Today, it is unlikely that a multi-ethnic society like America would fall victim to that same kind of vicious scapegoating perpetrated by the most virulent anti-Semites in Germany. Here, people will fight to protect their liberties; they will not give up their rights without a donnybrook of a struggle.

True, over many decades the United States frequently witnessed mob violence against black people; it took a large-scale civil rights movement to help change both attitudes and institutions as constitutional law evolved. In 1954 the old approach of "separate but equal" was struck down by the Supreme Court in *Brown v. Board of Education*. Incidents of racial hatred continued to occur, as they do to this day, but not the massive systematic discrimination and pervasive violence that once permeated the nation. Anti-Semitism still exists, too, but it would not be easy for anyone, even a charismatic politician like Donald Trump, to whip up a genocidal frenzy against Jews the way Hitler did in Germany.

We have always had anti-Semites here, of course, but they are relatively small in number compared to the law-abiding American majority which continues to increase in size and strength. It may not seem like much consolation after another anti-Semitic incident but we are speaking here of long-term patterns and not merely the intermittent and irrational descent into hatred that occasionally overwhelms the reason of an alienated loner or extremist ideologue.

Such hatred exists but we do not have an obsession with exterminating Jews, as Hitler did. We

26

do not have a national obsession with intimidating Black people or bringing back Jim Crow segregationist laws, as white supremacists might wish. It's possible that some of Trump's most fervent supporters would get behind him even if he unfurled a racist-fascist strategy, but not enough to matter. Any attempt by the GOP's Far Right to take a step toward declaring an entire people "inferior" and only fit for genocidal extermination would be met with the greatest outcry. Germany's story is not America's, thankfully!

Still, repeated steps by the Republican Party moving toward a right-wing ideology remains worrisome, for such a political reorientation seems wholly out of step with our nation's traditional democratic values and commitments. We know Trump has many of his most ardent supporters completely buffaloed; he has pulled the wool over their eyes so completely as to induce a kind of blindness while he and his wealthy supporters make the most of such loyalty: the blinder the better. They hide behind accountants and lawyers while millions of dollars sail into Trump's coffers as he tries to maintain the false claim he "won" the election. He didn't win but he *lied* that he did. How is such a man qualified to hold any public office ever again?[4]

---

[4] Perhaps, under Section 3 of the Fourteenth Amendment, he could be disqualified. (And if someone is reminded of the Big Lie propaganda technique of Adolf Hitler, how can that be helped?)

Trump blustered and threatened and threw one hissy-fit after another. Then the ultimate "threat": he was going to go to court to prove the election was stolen! That didn't end especially well for him, did it? Lawyers on his behalf brought sixty-three lawsuits concerning vote counting and certification procedures in nine different states. Nearly all cases were dropped or dismissed for lack of evidence. The courts have stringent standards that cannot be reduced or negated, bullied or bludgeoned, ignored or dismissed by the likes of Trump. He lost case after case, a stinging rebuke of his false posturing. America's biggest braggart got his inevitable comeuppance since his lawyers brought no credible evidence of anything fraudulent to the courtroom. Sixty-two attempts at "blowing legal smoke" were thrown out for lack of substance:[5]

"Only one ruling was initially in Trump's favor: the timing within which first-time Pennsylvania voters must provide proper identification if they wanted to 'cure' their ballots. This ruling affected very few votes, and it was later overturned by the Pennsylvania Supreme Court." (*Business Insider*, January 11, 2021). The nation held its breath in suspense since no one

---

[5] Of the sixty-three cases, he won a small victory; Republican observers would be allowed to stand a little closer to observe Philadelphia's poll workers. He lost all other cases because his fictional accusations did not play well in an American court of law with a long history of filtering out chaff from substance and weighing objectively tangible physical evidence.

initially knew how far the cases might proceed, and then it let out a collective sigh of relief to see the lack of substance exposed in each case. The legal drama took on an element of farce when even his attorneys got in trouble: "Federal judge sanctions Trump attorneys for spreading false election fraud claims."[6] How weak is one's legal position when a judge has to chastise your appointed lawyers for engaging in unethical conduct?

The courts were not under Trump's control; in the courtroom all his false claims amounted to less than nothing. Perhaps he was not playing with a full deck and his obsessive narcissistic personality drove him forward; perhaps he simply realized that cash would keep rolling in from his supporters as long as he cried foul while challenging the election outcome. He has a backwards Midas knack for using other people's money to get what he wants and this situation was no exception: everything he touches turns to dirt, not gold. He stayed with the charade as long as he could until the ethereal nature of his false claims finally dissipated into thin air. He got nowhere in the courts because he could not produce a shred of evidence. Where all the money he raised is going, is another question yet to be determined.

Certainly, it is not inconceivable that a so-called "strong man" might arise in this country one day, not unlike the dictators of South America and elsewhere,

---

[6] **https://www.nbcnews.com/politics/politics-news/federal-judge-sanctions-trump-attorneys-spreading-false-election-fraud-claims-n1277664** retrieved 11/21/22.

but the United States has a different history and culture. Central and South American nations have known authoritarian regimes for most of their modern national histories yet here there is a successful democratic tradition that is more than two hundred years old. South American countries have floundered under dictatorial one-man rule; it is not a surprise when a Central or South American nation succumbs to takeover by military dictatorship. By contrast, American democracy has grown ever more vibrant by trusting self-government and unleashing the potential of its people: intellectual, scientific, and technological.

America remains the premier example of a democratic nation in the modern era. Its pledge and surety is found in the *Constitution*, in the conduct of its elected representatives, and most of all in the lives and character of its people; ultimately, our democracy is guarded by millions of Americans. They are not to be fooled or intimidated into giving up their rights through the devious ploys of charlatans and would-be authoritarian figures. The nation has a wide range of offices and institutions with decision-making power wisely spread throughout the three branches of government, each charged with protecting those rights. Our legislative and judicial branches are especially well-suited to exercising their duties and responsibilities in an ethical and mandated manner. Through daily life and measured decorum, both the government and the people themselves give form and substance to the democratic precepts first expressed by the Founding Fathers.

Although the wheels of legislative and judicial processes may at times seem to turn distressingly slow, history bears witness to one simple fact: the people have always kept faith with the principles of America's birthright and never more so than when the challenge is the greatest. When fascism threatened the world, American men and women showed the courage and determination to keep freedom safe; they made the necessary sacrifices to defeat Hitler. They have kept civil society moving steadily forward along the promised path of freedom, justice, and equality. Despite unseemly chapters in our nation's past, the lofty ideals of the Declaration of Independence remain living sentiments which generations of Americans have kept close to their hearts.

Compare America to the Axis powers of World War II: Germany, Italy, and Japan. What democratic precepts and practices did the German people have? After Paul von Hindenburg appointed Hitler as Chancellor, the German people were left with a Fuehrer's manic obsession with Jews, Slavs, and Bolsheviks; the nation's "foreign policy" was based on Hitler's intent to rely on slave labor and genocide while seeking world conquest. He ultimately subjected his country to Allied massive attacks and catastrophic devastation, involving utter ruin on a hitherto unimaginable scale. Major German cities were reduced to rubble as part of that widespread destruction. There was naught of the honorable or fair-minded in Hitler;

ethical leadership is found in democracies and not dictatorships.

Built into our nation's foundation principles, one finds a level of conscience and responsibility among individuals that only constitutional republics establish and demand. Looking back, Germany had Otto Bismarck and Kaiser Wilhelm as rulers; Bismarck favored monarchy and the divine right of kings while Kaiser Wilhelm, as an autocratic ruler, leaned toward dictatorial methods. The people of the United States have the lives and words of men like Thomas Jefferson and Abraham Lincoln from whom to draw inspiration and a deeper commitment to constitutional and democratic ideals.

Americans may read with pride the words of these two men, from "All men are created equal" in Jefferson's Declaration of Independence to Lincoln's Emancipation Proclamation: "...all persons held as slaves within any State...the people whereof shall then be in rebellion against the United States, shall be then, thenceforward, and *forever free...*" The colonists fought to free their new country from England, Jefferson explained the reasons why, and Lincoln delivered the death blow against slavery. We have a long history of courageous soldiers and wise statesmen to give meaning to our birthright and existence. They created the momentum for further growth across the generations, derived from the fundamental nature of our principles and national character.

That Germany once succumbed to Nazism does not mean other countries, including the United States, will turn to fascism, too. The horrors of Hitler and World War II are too deeply embedded in the psyche of Americans and all the peoples of the world to allow Nazism to take hold. It is unlikely that democratic nations will let a new Hitler plunge the world into war again. By the same token, however, Americans must not get overconfident. Because Germany had fascism "a long time ago" does not mean fascism cannot reappear, perhaps in some unsuspecting country. Could it happen here? That depends in large measure on how vigilant and well-informed the American people demonstrate themselves to be.

A strange combination of events made Hitler's toppling of the Weimar Republic possible. He organized a "putsch" in Munich which failed miserably; he could have been stopped there if the political desire to do so had existed. Hitler was found guilty of treason and sentenced to five years in prison but was released after only nine months. He eventually found another path forward to fascism, to rule for twelve years the "Reich" that was to last a thousand years. Historians and biographers focus today a good deal on the personality of a man like Hitler but we must not forget that much larger social and economic forces were at play as well; wealthy industrialists who backed his Nazi program allowed him to get much farther than he would have been able to do otherwise.

Today, there remains a chance that some of Trump's most right-wing supporters might try to move the nation toward fascism; you wouldn't think so but we cannot dismiss it out of hand as impossible, either. The dark money keeps flowing from pocket to pocket and from purse to purse, from the bank accounts of wealthy donors to the overflowing campaign cash reserves of the Republican Party. Given enough monetary backing, there is no telling what role Trump might play in undermining American democracy in order to replace it with something more authoritarian. Many of his utterances have been criticized as condescending, foolish, and outlandish by journalists, especially when compared to the level-headed conduct of previous presidents. Trump, however, is also surprisingly devious and calculating, enough so that he must be considered more than just a clown or cult leader. *No one should underestimate the real and present danger he poses to constitutional democracy.*

Americans are free to examine for themselves the platforms of the Democratic and Republican parties. At the same time, they must be careful not to turn a blind eye regarding the sly way the Republicans have been gerrymandering and passing restrictive voting laws, making it harder for some people to vote and, inversely, easier for their candidates to succeed. This is a "legal strategy" engineered by the GOP to win elections. It is anti-democratic and an obvious play for power when they cannot win by fair means. We must never forget about the dangers of fascism arising but, in the here and now, we must be equally concerned that The GOP is looking for ways to win elections by any means available, especially when its candidates are unable to secure an honest popular majority.

What is that but cheating? These tactics of the Republican Party's Far Right are implemented so the GOP candidate can claim victory by means fair or foul. Trump's Big Lie that the election was stolen is truly reminiscent of Hitler's fascist propaganda in Germany, setting a dubious precedent for future forays toward an authoritarian mindset. There is much to concern us here regarding the Grand Old Party itself, in addition to the unpredictable behavior of Donald J. Trump and the angry militants he unleashes from time to time.

On one level, "I won the election" is just another piece of his public stage performance where he forces the whole country to focus on him, even though, *factually*, every reasonable person knows he lost. On another level, however, his bogus claim can be seen as part of a wider effort to undermine democracy itself, a harbinger of right-wing tactics spinning out of control. Is it crazy, yes; is it funny, perhaps a little; but the real question remains: could it mask another dangerous shift to the Far Right? Absolutely!

****

Party Platforms

In general, the Republicans represent the idea of letting each individual or family (each business or corporation) do as well as it can for itself with as little government influence as possible.[7] Most Democrats have a different starting point; they take the view that *all* Americans should share in the progress and wealth of the nation. They defend certain principles and values, based on their understanding of the Constitution and the American Revolution, out of whose trials and tribulations our fundamental document was born.

During the Great Depression, the Democrats in Congress, led by Franklin Delano Roosevelt, took swift action to save the collapsing economy; American lives were increasingly endangered by the lack of income and other hardships introduced by the crisis. FDR tried to limit the negative effects of the Stock Market's plunge and sought a way forward out of the crisis. When war clouds darkened the horizon, especially after the Japanese attack on Pearl Harbor, the Democrats led the fight against the fascist aggressors in both Europe and the Pacific. Once the Republicans got back in power in the 1950s, however, they started moving the country to the right. They opposed the policies and precepts Franklin Delano Roosevelt had represented.

---

[7] From time to time the reader might hear the allegation of "corporate welfare" but we must save that discussion for another time and place.

The New Deal had far too much "socialism" for the conservatives, especially the right-wing of the Republican Party; it was the gravity of the economic crisis during the Great Depression that had forced them to keep quiet for fear of social upheaval and revolution.

Voters today may be inspired by many different issues to support one party or the other and may judge for themselves the intelligence and character of each candidate. Southern whites who opposed equality for African-Americans were Democrats until the 1960's when many moved over to the Republican Party. The Republicans have fared well in the Midwest among American farmers and those groups who prize "rugged individualism." One can further sort demographic differences between the two parties by gender, class, race, region, and even hot-button cultural issues: abortion access, legislative response to mass shootings, teaching of Black history, LGBTQ rights, book censorship, etc. What is written here is intended as generalization and is primarily concerned with the role money plays in influencing election outcomes for the two major parties. In this sense, the Republican Party fares quite well among the wealthy. This might appear to give them an unfair advantage over the Democrats since campaigns are increasingly becoming a contest of money-vs-money. The Republican Party with its "deep pockets" appears to have a bottomless treasury; they can afford to spend millions of dollars on multiple campaigns.

In close elections, wealthy Republican leaders and stalwarts may even use some of their own funds to buy air time to attack Democratic opponents and to pump up their party's candidates. Smear campaigns have become common for some types of Republican candidates. Keeping a civil tongue in one's head and letting one's character speak for itself seems less likely in every new election cycle. Yet there is a considerable moral difference between honest criticism and dishonest posturing, a line that seems to be getting constantly blurred by right-wing Republicans.

A certain type of Republican candidate turns to the tactics of sly innuendos and false accusations, just for the sensationalism and temporary gain of the moment. Unfortunately, Republican-appointed justices to the Supreme Court have turned their honorable institution into a conservative battering ram in its own right. Talk of abstract principles of equality and justice are all well and good, but in the here and now Republican leaders are congratulating themselves on having "captured" the Supreme Court.

In 2010 the Supreme Court's ruling in *Citizens United v. Federal Election Commission* overturned an earlier case from 1990 that allowed some restrictions on corporate spending in election campaigns. Essentially, there would now be no limits since the Court chose to interpret campaign contributions as a form of free speech; attempts by states to encourage financial transparency also suffered a grievous setback at the same time. Since dark money could now be kept dark, the richest families and corporations in the country were free to give large sums of money to any candidate (including right-wing extremists) and keep it secret.

Sometimes the Supreme Court appears to forget where its constitutional obligation to preserve democracy should be; sometimes they lead and sometimes they lag behind, as they did in this instance. The conservative Justices made a fundamental blunder in interpreting the First Amendment as protecting "dark money;" unfortunately, it will no doubt be a long time before a new Court can address and remedy the error.

Over the last few decades Republican leaders have pursued the goal of getting GOP-approved conservative Justices appointed to the Court whenever an opening arose under a Republican president and the tactic now seems to be bearing fruit. The leadership has kept track of judicial appointments and philosophical leanings for quite some time; they have a list of the judges they wish to see appointed to the higher courts. Rather than supporting the best legal minds in the country as nominees, Republican presidents sought out nominees who shared the GOP's conservative philosophy.[8]

The candidates chosen for the short list were questioned and vetted in a new way, with a litmus-type test applied in selecting individuals with the correct ideological position on abortion, gun rights, DACA

---

[8] The Federalist Society helps produce a list of conservative judges to fill vacancies at all levels. They favored Neil Gorsuch for the Supreme Court, who was nominated by Trump.

(Deferred Action for Childhood Arrivals), immigrants, and so forth. The GOP would block any nominee's confirmation if he or she supported a woman's right to choose. The candidate would have to meet the party's expectations in this and other areas. These matters are not addressed quite so openly, of course; the candidates for the Supreme Court typically refuse to say whether they are for or against any issue before a specific case is presented to them. Yet the GOP short list only includes those candidates whose experiences and legal opinions tell the keepers of the list which ones are conservative enough to be worth advancing.

Instead of seeking out the best legal minds, the most brilliant scholars when it comes to understanding the Constitution, the GOP seeks out individuals who subscribe to their conservative philosophy and goals. In doing so, they inject partisan factionalism into the highest court of the land, making the Supreme Court into a political football to be captured or controlled by a right-wing faction within the Republican Party. Taking the long view, such an approach risks great harm to the country, yet this tactical commitment of the GOP remains ever present. In March 2016 Speaker McConnell shocked the nation by refusing to give President Obama's choice, Merrick Garland, the hearing owed him, based on which the Senate approves or disapproves of a president's nominee. The Speaker's unprecedented unilateral action went far beyond his powers and how the Constitution describes the process.

McConnell claimed the proper procedure was to wait months for the next election when nothing in the

Constitution supports such a position. McConnell's rationalization was nothing more than a cover for the improper procedure he made up, motivated solely by a desire to help increase the conservative majority on the nation's highest Court. *In effect, he suspended the Constitution and acted in a manner entirely contrary to its stated purposes.* By so doing, McConnell helped the Republicans construct another approach for opposing or undoing Democratic nominations. Today, if Congress passes laws not to the GOP's liking, the Republicans have substantially increased the likelihood of a conservative Supreme Court taking action to modify or stop the new laws. Such action is not guaranteed but its probability has changed in their favor.

If this criticism seems unfair, consider for a moment the flip-flop McConnell performed after the passing of Ruth Bader Ginzburg. He had already publicly asserted that President Obama's nominee to the Supreme Court, Merrick Garland, would not get a hearing; he made the assertion *eleven months* before the 2016 election. Obama announced his decision in March 2016, *eight months* before the November election and true to his word McConnell prevented the Senate from considering the nomination. He hoped that by waiting nearly a year, the Republican Party could win the presidency and control the process for filling the vacant Supreme Court seat.

However, when Ruth Bader Ginzburg died on September 18, 2020, just *two months* before the next election, McConnell allowed the Senate to vote right away on the nomination of Amy Coney Barrett on September 26. This contradiction between word and deed demonstrated a hypocrisy that could not be more flagrant. McConnell's actions revealed that his word was not to be trusted: that he would practice no consistency in applying constitutional rules and obligations in the Senate regarding Supreme Court nominees. He was practicing a form of *realpolitik*, associated with the name Otto von Bismarck, Iron Chancellor of Germany. Such an approach minimizes ethical considerations in favor of achieving pragmatic goals, even at the expense of honesty of character and conscience.

The Democrats often do well among unions, working people, students and minorities; the party also has its share of big money donors but they typically are not as influential, numerous, or as flamboyant as the fabulously wealthy donors for the GOP, like the Koch brothers.[9] For some time past, great wealth has tended to favor the elephant, symbol of the Republican Party. Of course, the GOP also has support among segments of the middle class and the working class; not all Republicans are rich. We must not forget those men and women who are attracted to the GOP by the

---

[9] Charles and David Koch, two rich conservatives; David passed away in August 2019. Other wealthy backers include gambling mogul Sheldon Adelson, Stephen Schwarzman, Diane Hendricks, Texas banker Andy Beal, and casino king Phil Ruffin. *Forbes* found that 133 billionaires supported Trump's candidacy.

"culture wars" and hot-button issues like gun rights, abortion, immigration, school curriculum, the banning of certain books, etc. Yet the ordinary "not very rich" Republican cannot influence an election outcome in the same way as the party's biggest donors, with their contributions of millions of dollars.

"Individualism" as a philosophy has an attractive quality to it, buttressed by patriotic rhetoric and chauvinistic attitudes toward minorities and immigrants. When John F. Kennedy supported the civil rights movement, the southern Dixiecrats,

formerly Democrats, began gravitating toward the GOP; the Republicans established a strong presence in any number of southern states. Both parties see rivers of money flow in and out for campaign purposes; it is one of the reasons GOP candidates often gravitate toward controversial issues and outlandish claims, in order to generate the most generous financial support.

In general, it is believed that the Republican Party has more millionaire-billionaire "sugar daddies" (extremely rich backers) than the Democrats who must rely on broader mass support: money versus number of people, as it were. Until relatively recently, liberals and conservatives had plenty to say to each other and did so as part of a healthy debate within a democratic framework. Now of course the parties are barely civil to one another; the GOP has developed a well-earned reputation as the "party of no!" in reference to any ideas the Democratic Party might propose.

In the twenty-first century, we must ask: is this "normal bickering" or could such tensions worsen to the point where the Republican right-wing moves toward fascism? It is unlikely at this time, given the circumstances alluded to elsewhere in this work.[10] There are other factors limiting this push to the right; neo-Nazis may march and shout anti-Semitic slogans but the America of today is not the Germany of Hitler. Perhaps the United States will start moving in that direction, perhaps not; it seems unlikely that democratic-minded Americans would allow a man like Trump (or any other) to turn American society into an outright dictatorship.

That is not to say there is no danger ahead for America, for surely there is. It is merely to remind everyone that the economic conditions today are much different than the circumstances of the 1930's; moreover, the moral and political resolve of the American people has matured considerably in the last seventy-five years. America's civil rights movement has transformed our society in ways that cannot be easily undone; the United States today is not the same as Nazi Germany under Hitler. Anyone who attempts to create a fascist state here would no doubt face a prolonged and titanic opposition.

While it remains worrisome that the Republican Party has become so ultra-conservative that it tolerates white supremacists, there is a limit to their movement in that direction. The more GOP leaders express their

---

[10] See the preceding essay, "Trump the Notorious Liar".

sympathy for racist views, the more support they risk losing. The United States is a multi-cultural society made up of people of many diverse backgrounds; America has great diversity when it comes to religion and ethnicity. There are many kinds of neighborhoods with a unique culture in food, music, art and dance. It is one of the glories of American democracy that we have such a diverse and open society.

White chauvinism is never completely absent but it is weakening. Its most extreme form, lynching, is more a phenomenon of the past than the present; not even diehard racists can turn back the hands of time. Racists who bemoan the passing of the "good old days" may engage in delaying tactics but the nation's progress toward justice and equality cannot be stopped. The British monarchy could not prevent the American Revolution; the French aristocracy could not quash the French Revolution. The planter class of the Old South could not prevent the abolition of slavery; in the twentieth century the rabid segregationists in southern states could not stop the civil rights movement and its clarion call to put an end to segregation. As for fascism, the Nazis could not defeat the Allies, representing the combined forces of many freedom-loving nations and peoples.

These are historic movements whose time has come; conservatives and reactionaries may fight against all such social change but they are not on the right side of history. Trump's base might get excited over the prospect of him as a new kind of presidential "fuehrer"

45

but I speak here of the electoral losses that are likely to occur all across the country if the GOP succumbs to the Far Right and follows an unpredictable narcissist to the bitter end. In 2020 Trump lost multiple swing states; indeed, he provoked a growing number of people, spread throughout the nation, to turn against him. Is the GOP too dull to grasp that? Or will a more moderate voice emerge? If the Republican Party sees Trump as a loser and shoves him aside, will they return to "normal conservatism" or will they continue their party's right-wing transformation? Are they already on an irreversible downward slide about to go past the point of no return?

If the GOP becomes even more rightwing than it already is, it will continue to lose large swaths of support; thousands of Republicans will abandon the sinking ship while the Democrats and Independents close ranks in a common cause. The GOP can't go much farther to the Right without coming to the final fork in the road; it must return to the fold or become a proto-fascist menace. Which way will the current Republican leadership wish to go? It is difficult to tell since they have been tolerating right-wing spokesmen for so long; it is devoutly to be wished they will become a respectable party again with specific goals and policies, democratic and constitutional in nature, inspired to meet the needs of the American people and not hatched merely to increase the wealth of the top one percent of the country.

Furthermore, GOP leaders must be ready to apply some degree of restraint on anyone among them who strays too close to fascism. Will the GOP make such a pledge? Why are they slow to condemn rightwing views and activities that are an unmistakable threat to American democracy? *Are the current leaders planning to fold and let their party be transformed into a clique run by racists and neo-fascists?* Are they ready to give up on nearly two hundred and fifty years of a constitutional republic in favor of one-man rule: that of Trump or someone like him as a successor?

It is possible that the nation may be headed for a period of unrest with large-scale social disturbances and, beyond, perhaps encountering the first harbingers of civil war. If that kind of violence occurs in our nation's future, it will come when it does and not before: that is, when antagonistic social elements have reached a point of no return, ushering in a collision of values and beliefs that cannot be avoided. If, finally, Americans begin to shoot at one another with lethal intent, then we will have to concede that, despite our best efforts, the ugly specter of civil war will have found a way to darken America's horizon once more.

Historical forces larger than either party may have the final say in what is to befall America. However, this scenario of racial or class warfare does not need to happen and remains unlikely, at least in the near future. After all, Lincoln's "common people" greatly outnumber the "rich and famous" with their fingers in too many pies. I daresay the wealthy have more to fear from a violent conflagration than do ordinary Americans, who have less to lose. Conflict over dwindling resources (water, energy) might become one cause of open conflict; racial antagonisms another.

It is noteworthy that the author can get this far in suggesting the possibility of civil war and still have readers follow his reasoning, as perhaps they should. Even idle speculation, if that is all this proves to be, may find relevance in the future. But does it not say something about the nature of Trump's destructive and divisive influence that an essay that began with a simple critique of his narcissism and penchant for falsehoods can end up discussing the possibility of civil war, brought about by his actions and beliefs?

Yes, the danger of an authoritarian personality at the head of our government does exist; the danger of creeping fascism is perhaps reaching a new level of influence with its invidious presence. Whenever a president ignores or bends well-established presidential obligations, protocols, and traditions beyond recognition, democracy suffers grievously as a result. Whenever a president ceases doing his duty to protect fundamental constitutional principles as his highest priority, the danger from the Far Right increases exponentially. Trump not only ignored presidential etiquette and expectations but he deliberately defied constitutional limits on his power, leading to not one but two impeachments.

Worse yet, he sparked a violent insurrection in the nation's capital; he tolerated it for hours and refused to condemn it in a manner worthy of the office of an American president. Later, he hinted that if the insurrectionists were arrested and convicted, he would consider granting pardons: *pardons for violent felons who attacked Congress and law enforcement officers; pardons for rioters who attempted to overturn the results of a free election and thus struck at the very heart of American democracy itself!*

Wealthy conservative elites (whom we don't always get to see on a daily basis) undoubtedly enjoy having a taboo-busting real-estate tycoon like Trump do their bidding; they are just licking their chops. The Republican Party and their richest donors would like to get this man back in office in 2024 but they must first soberly assess his performance and reputation, not just with his base but with the rest of the nation as well. It's a pickle of a dilemma for rightwingers, figuring out when to push harder the ideology of the Far Right and when to stay put. It is a sad commentary on the state of current affairs to note that by merely watching the GOP, Americans can figure out which way the Winds of Reaction are blowing.

If the Republican Party has already been captured by right-wing elements intent on never relinquishing their hold, as seems to be true at the present time, the American people will at least have time to prepare for future crises the GOP will cause. Ever since our Revolution, the American people have understood what it means for a citizen to behave lawfully and ethically. And yet, if ever they must fight fire with fire, they will ready themselves for that possibility, too. They are not likely to give away the democratic country that so many hard-working generations of Americans have worked to build, from Washington to Biden. As Jefferson said:

"The price of liberty is eternal vigilance."

It is this generation's turn to stand vigil.

****

NEVER AGAIN!

Perhaps the dark money contributors are looking for Donald to stick his head out the window and see how far he can get with his ludicrous fairy-tales; if he is not careful, he will get it knocked off. Trying to overturn an election has not gone unnoticed by millions of Americans. Anyone who tries to rig or steal an election is surely not acting in the best interests of the nation. He no doubt lost a great deal of respect among many Americans, even those who once supported him; as for those who already opposed him, his reputation sank beneath the waves.

The older generation remembers that at the end of World War II the single most important anti-fascist slogan to emerge was: "NEVER AGAIN!" A war like that provides for long memories, even generations. The Nazis ended free elections in Germany. The fascists depended heavily on brute force and coercive conformity rather than allowing citizens to express their opinions through free elections and a free press. In hindsight, during the 1930s one of the biggest mistakes the Allied Nations made was waiting too long to confront Hitler when he began rebuilding the German Army, in violation of the Treaty of Versailles. Hitler took over the Ruhr Valley and then the Rhineland (1936); he gobbled up Czechoslovakia's Sudetenland (1938).

England's Neville Chamberlain (he of England's Conservative Party) naively thought he had successfully "appeased" Hitler in September 1938, a policy which Winston Churchill promptly called "an unmitigated disaster". The Nazi leader was only biding his time; Hitler took over more of Czechoslovakia the following year and became the twentieth century's poster-boy for fascist dictatorship. That dreadful prospect, of a dictator taking control of a country is a fearful and sometimes lethal reality, experienced by people around the world. Many know from their own experiences that whenever a murderous and ruthless dictator takes over, it means "farewell to freedom" and "hello to prison chains and gallows."

In the United States, however, there exists a liberty-loving patriotism that runs as deep here as anywhere in the world. The Far Right won't find it easy to locate an obsessive anti-Semitic corporal like Hitler to try and take over the USA and its military; perhaps that's why the right-wing of the GOP had to look elsewhere and settle for someone like Trump. The current GOP leaders do not appear ready to turn their backs on him in order to embrace the stability and sanity of a more moderate Republicanism; they are moving at a snails' pace to recognize the urgent need for the party to return to its traditional base and away from rightwing conspiracy theorists and other extremists.

Trump and company still appear to exercise firm control over the minds of most members of their party, yet it should be remembered that this latest "sprint to the right" did not bubble up as popular pressure from the rank-and-file. Rather, a wealthy elite combined with right-wing ideologues to determine where the party should be headed next; billionaires ended up backing one of their own, another billionaire. Endorsing Trump turned out to be a shuffle so far to the right that nothing more is to be found in that direction but neo-fascist rhetoric, which has begun to increase noticeably in tenor and volume in recent years.

Casting doubt on a presidential election introduces a slippery slope. Historically, Republicans and Democrats have had their policy differences but they also competed fairly in open forums, often alternating turns in the White House as the American people voted first for one party and then the other. It is one of the great strengths of our country that we have a two-party system wherein both parties uphold principles of freedom and conscience while differing on policy issues. Americans have a choice in their candidates; they retain the basic right of suffrage, to vote in a free and open election by secret ballot.

After the end of segregation and black disenfranchisement in the South in the 1960's, neither party argued that the best way to win an election was to see how many voters could be disenfranchised; new laws and attitudes had finally combined to put an end to the suppression of suffrage for African-Americans. Neither party advocated the re-establishment of the poll tax, literacy tests, and so on; nearly every American recognized that the civil rights movement achieved significant change and that those good old days of "whites only" were on their way out.

The current GOP, on the other hand, has once again begun to engage in voter suppression efforts to ensure they can finagle their way back into power; with all their heavy-handed moves the danger of a one-party state comes one step closer to realization. If Republicans are successful in "winning" an election where their candidate did not achieve a true majority, aren't they the ones trying to steal an election: steal one, why not another? Only time will tell but that danger appears real and ever-present.

The GOP leaders began abandoning certain policies long ago; I would say the brain drain began in the 1950s but other historians will lambast such a caustic attitude, admonishing me that I must move my timetable up to *at least Richard Nixon*. With him, many writers are willing to admit there was a Republican administration that ushered in a steep decline for presidential ethics. Reagan, however, remains a hero with the Far Right *despite his tripling of the national debt*; he deregulated industries and pursued anti-union policies that hurt workers in order to satisfy the demands of his big money backers, especially those who profited most handsomely by such deregulation and union-busting. Reagan fired more than 11,000 striking air traffic controllers, a serious blow to the labor movement. The Iran-Contra affair, an illegal enterprise from start to finish, was conducted in the basement of the White House where he was living but he "hadn't a clue" that it was happening, supposedly.[11] A comedian named Jackie Mason developed an entire routine making audiences roar with laughter over the improbable and sometimes absurd nature of Reagan's explanations.

Personally, I think the Republican Party began moving away from moderation as early as the 1950s. They hoped no one would notice their slide to the right since the shift would not fully materialize for years. The richest Republicans already controlled much of the business life of the country; their candidates' attitude usually included "don't rock the boat." In stealth they moved forward but they were not entirely prepared for what happened next. The generation of the Sixties turned things topsy-turvy with the young people condemning the hypocrisy and double-dealing, lies and myths that kept politicians in office.

That decade must not be seen in isolation or as some inexplicable social phenomenon. It was nothing less than a repudiation of the status quo of the 1950s; it was the new generation's rejection of the stifling

---

[11] The German Army was limited to 100,000 soldiers. The manufacture of various weapons was forbidden, including tanks, airplanes, armored vehicles, submarines, and poison gas; the general staff was eliminated. It sounded good on paper but was not enforced once Hitler took power.

conformist drivel being served up as pap in newspapers and on television for far too long. There was a revolution in mindset that accelerated rapidly among young people; their heightened sense of conscience refused to make peace with racism, militarism, exploitation, and poverty. Great leaders arose but they were shot down one by one: Medgar Evers in Mississippi, John F. Kennedy in Dallas, his brother Robert F. Kennedy in Los Angeles, Malcolm X in New York City and even the great apostle of non-violence, Dr. Martin Luther King, Jr. in Memphis, Tennessee. What a depth and range of intellect was lost with the tragic and untimely deaths of these men!

They were the cream of the crop; Dr. King was the kind of extraordinary philosopher, preacher, and civil rights leader who appears but once in a lifetime. Despite the devastating losses caused by their deaths, popular movements for change re-focused their energies and grew stronger; college students and community activists have been making great strides in transforming America. The movement was no longer based on the goals of any one leader; the movement was based on a grassroots ground-swell demanding justice. During the Sixties, the Republicans became the forerunners of the current "just say no" Republican Party that spends more time opposing Democratic proposals than it does in creating viable alternatives. The old leaders offered some nice-sounding rhetoric but beneath it was an iron fist of opposition to all progressive pieces of legislation aimed at helping minorities and the less fortunate.

At some point, the pundits couldn't help but nickname the GOP the "party of no;" the Republicans were becoming the party of distraction and misdirection. The GOP openly became the party of wealthy individuals and corporations (with an oversized influence on the finances of the country) while displaying minimum concern in helping ordinary Americans, especially if it should cut into their hoarded millions. Not just lip service, mind you, but real programs to reduce poverty and enlarge the middle class. Millionaires and billionaires have plans of their own; this unseemly worship of the dollar was bound to come back to haunt them.

At one time unions had been the backbone of the middle class; workers fought for union recognition in order to achieve safer working conditions, a living wage ("a fair day's wage for a fair day's labor"), health care, unemployment insurance, a retirement package, and other benefits. Even during the bleakest years for working-class families, many companies and corporations continued to make millions of dollars in profit. A good portion of the richest individuals and businesses somehow managed to survive both recession and depression while the common man was thrown out of work. The owners of mines, mills, and factories took notice of the strong union movement, with the Republican Party supporting anti-union policies. The auto plants began closing as owners shipped jobs overseas to take advantage of cheap labor and weak rules governing working conditions and environmental protection: a laxity which allowed enormous toxic discharges that poisoned land, air, and water. The notion of one earth, of global responsibility, was not in their vocabulary so long as their present set-up kept producing large-scale profits.

The Republicans, as the party of business and wealth, risk bankrupting themselves morally; over the years they kept shifting to the right until there was nowhere else to turn and only some form of authoritarian rule remained. An astute observer can see that their political thinking under Trump has become even more extreme and bears watching. Trump's bogus claim that the 2020 election was "rigged" was itself unprecedented in American history; he dared cast aspersions on Americans' honesty and on the fundamental democratic procedures of the nation itself.

Most Americans were shocked by January 6th and Trump's false claims; most of them had never seen such a gigantic "Whale of a Lie" coming from an embittered self-centered narcissist who once held the highest office in the land. It was stunning to realize that the White House had been occupied by a pathological liar and potential insurrectionist, as had been feared all along: a man who would attack an America's election rather than concede defeat when the results made it clear *that it was he who had lost and lost big, by over seven million votes.*[12]

---

[12] Final vote for Biden: 81,283,501 For Trump: 74,223,975. That's a difference of 7,059,526.

Whether his reputation will fall apart further or whether he will become the Republican Party's nominee in 2024 remains undecided. Yet, regarding the threat of authoritarianism, we must remember this truth: the American people have now seen another side of Trump. They have had ample opportunity to take the measure of the man and note the glaring deficiencies of his character and personality. We struggled through four years of brazen Trumpism even before the last month of his term was topped off by a violent insurrection in the nation's capital: an invasion of the halls of Congress. His glossy headshots are relics of an earlier time; Americans are learning to look past suit and tie, his outward appearance and accoutrements, and see him for who he is: the man who tried anything and everything, even an insurrection, to overturn an election.

The American people have seen his petty jealousies, his self-serving denial of facts and his vindictive behavior toward others. What we have witnessed speaks volumes to the hitherto hidden and unseemly aspects of his self-absorbed character. It is safe to surmise that he will wish to take revenge on all who criticized him and on all those who accepted the indisputable fact that a majority of Americans elected Joe Biden president. To perpetuate his lust for power, he was willing to incite his followers to attack Congress itself! He is a colossal narcissist in every sense of the word. He is not only an unrepentant braggart but his unbridled arrogance spills forth from a man who had no

59

political experience when he ran for office; he appears to have only a tenuous grasp concerning the integrity of the presidency and virtually no commitment to the principles, protocols, and duties of the office: the office as described in the U.S. Constitution. *He has made himself a clear and present danger to American democracy.*

Yes, the American people must prepare for the possibility of more extreme behavior from Trump and the Far Right, including his cult-like base and other extremists beyond. We have witnessed how far Trump will go to bend or circumvent constitutional obligations and principles. Any candidate who refuses to abide by the results of a fair and free election is too deceitful and dishonest to countenance; indeed, he is the last person to ever be trusted with the reins of power again.

He and his cronies thought nothing of unleashing a mob to attack the Capitol Building; they assaulted uniformed policemen defending the perimeter and our nation's elected representatives, just then in the process of verifying the 2020 election. The pro-Trump mob endangered them all as it tried to prevent Congress from completing its vital task. The insurrectionists violently interfered with how our democratic government, constitutionally-empowered, is pledged to work! If Trump is re-elected, he most likely would feel empowered to indulge his penchant for vendettas, made up of equal parts of verbal attack and legal suit, as well as the ever-present threat of actual physical harm inflicted by one or more of his followers.

He would want to increase his power so he could exercise his personal spite while protecting his vested interests. After all, he appears to carry grudges with a marked ferocity. No doubt he would become madly vengeful and spend much time going after enemies. He would try to control Democrats and journalists while letting out of jail the insurrectionists who attacked the government of the United States. The ghost of Nixon will wrap its arms around him and encourage him to forego reason, civility, and emotional stability for the sake of petty revenge.

Trump forgets that the Constitution is the true protector of the American people, not him or his circle of billionaires and loyal white supremacists. Americans will not abandon the Constitution to suit the likes of him or his right-wing followers. The courts will hold fast, as will the military, along with countless other democratic offices and institutions, including schools and churches. The American people in their tens of millions will never be tricked or cajoled out of their democracy merely to please the insufferable ego of a heartless braggart! If he thinks the American people turned on him in 2020, he hasn't seen anything yet. He and his clique of billionaires may be rich but they never fooled a *majority* of the American people. He never won the popular vote in 2016. He will have to find this out the hard way once again; it will be a pleasure to see him rebuffed when "push comes to shove" as in 2020.

The unpleasant question remains: Will Trump become the first president to attempt to transition our country from a democratic to an authoritarian state? I don't believe he has a snowball's chance in hell of succeeding, if such be his purported role in history, but if he wishes to tangle, tell him to "bring it on" whenever he's ready for "We the People" can say with utmost American sincerity . . . .

"NEVER AGAIN!!"

(The solemn anti-fascist oath taken at the end of the world war against fascism)

****

"Legitimate Political Discourse"

Feb. 4, 2022
WASHINGTON —

The Republican Party on Friday officially declared the Jan. 6, 2021 attack on the Capitol and events that led to it "legitimate political discourse" . . . . [13]

Pardon me while I roll up my pants legs because there's a sea of muck spreading all around my feet. It comes from the apologists for the GOP trying to save face over what happened on January 6, 2021 which was a national disgrace. For the younger generation, I should explain: the motion, mock or real, of rolling up one's pants legs was a clever way to indicate that what one was about to hear would be bull-shit (pardon my French!)

It anticipates a speaker's attempt to invent a far-fetched excuse to explain away something really stupid. My own father was a master of this pantomime, imparting to it a quite comical twist. He would put on his best innocent face when he suspected a phony-baloney

---

[13]https://www.nytimes.com/2022/02/04/us/politics/republicans-jan-6-cheney-censure.html

Retrieved on 11/25/22.

excuse was on its way and cry out "Wait, wait!" followed by a highly exaggerated act of rolling up his pants legs followed by "Okay, I'm ready!"

In real life, if there is water or mud that one must wade through a person might do exactly this as it is intended to keep the bottom part of one's pants clean but of course my dad was offering a skeptical judgment: here comes a story too improbable to believe! As soon as the Republican Party offered this three-word phrase "legitimate political discourse" to excuse the January 6 Riot, I knew it was time "to roll up my pants" to avoid stepping in a liar's sea of muck.

Let us look at the three-word expression more closely, relying on time-honored definitions so we can examine the lexical meaning of each term, as well as any associated connotations, especially the first and most debatable term: "legitimate." Next, we will examine the word's antonyms so we can complete our understanding through an appreciation of the word's exact opposite. In this manner, we should be able to develop a stronger sense of whether these three terms, forged together in this curious way, are being used correctly or deceptively.

Here's a heads up: look for definitions that include the concept of "lawful" for legitimate.

Ask yourself, what does that term, legitimate, have to do with the unlawful January 6th riot and insurrection?

- Do these three words honestly describe the events of that tumultuous day?
- Was it lawful to commit multiple felonies?

The GOP that once proudly proclaimed itself the party of law and order, now stands silent as millions of Americans try to absorb the horrendous events of that day; true patriots were shaken to their core.

LEGITIMATE:

The word can be used as an adjective or verb.

As an adjective:
1. According to law; lawful: *the property's legitimate owner.*
2. In accordance with established rules, principles, or standards.

As a verb (used with object):
1. To make lawful or legal; pronounce or state as lawful.
2. To establish as lawfully born.

Synonyms conveying the same approximate meaning: legal, sanctioned, valid, legalize, etc.

Antonyms include: illegitimate, unsanctioned, criminal, unethical, unjustified, etc.

POLITICAL
Adjective
1. Concerned with **politics**: *political writers.*
2. Connected with a political party: *a political campaign.*

3. Exercising or seeking power in the governmental or public affairs of a state, municipality, etc.: *a political machine; a political boss.*
4. Involving the state or its government: *a political offense.*
5. Having a definite policy or system of government: *a political community.*
6. Of or relating to citizens: *political rights.*

(The term "political" is such common vocabulary it does not require further commentary).

DISCOURSE
Noun
1. Communication of thought by words; talk; conversation: earnest and intelligent discourse.
2. A formal discussion of a subject in speech or writing, as a dissertation, treatise, sermon, etc.

Verb (used without object)
1. To communicate thoughts orally; talk; converse.
2. To treat of a subject formally in speech or writing.

Opposite concepts: shouting match, tirade, angry speech, etc. "Discourse" tends to suggest a high level of reasoning and writing, of respecting the intellectual prowess of the other side, as well as one's own.

The January 6th riot involved a rampaging mob that committed multiple acts of trespass and vandalism as well as the more serious crimes of assault and insurrection, all aimed at preventing the verification of a presidential election. It was most likely organized by Trump supporters, right-wing extremists not averse to violence who were misled into accepting Trump's Big

Lie. The protestors attacked law enforcement officers, beating and injuring men in uniform; these men were ordinary citizens fulfilling their duty by protecting the Capitol, including the safety of elected government officials. Where was the discourse? Where was the intelligent exchange of ideas?

The philosopher Jean-Jacques Rousseau authored an essay entitled *A Discourse on the Moral Effects of the Arts and Sciences* (1750). Here the word "discourse" in the title conveys a proper sense of the essay being a serious and intelligent expression of ideas: not glib or rambling speech or violent exhortation to riot and mayhem. Compare the literary efforts of philosophers like Rousseau with what the rioters yelled during the insurrection. They shouted racial slurs at African-Americans, especially the "n" word; they aimed their virulent hate speech at black officers in uniform who were risking their lives to protect American democracy. The rioters engaged in many instances of bigoted and vulgar speech; Trump's racist supporters could not keep their racism in check. Additionally, they threatened lives with their violent assaults and calls to action like "Hang Mike Pence!"

That is the mentality and speech of a lynch mob; that is the reckless behavior of rioters intent on breaking the law and physically attacking anyone who got in their way. That is not intelligent *discourse* but riotous speech and criminal behavior; there is no fair exchange of ideas and certainly no reasonable dialogue based on peaceful persuasion.

- In looking at all the violent actions of that day, in assessing the crowd's behavior, what was "legitimate"?
- Where was the lawful exercise of the right to peacefully assemble?

Look again at the euphemistic phrase "legitimate political discourse" the GOP conjures up to excuse the seditious rampage at the Capitol Building. Is this not an attempt to throw sand in the eyes of the American people? What unmitigated gall! Do we not have the right to roll up our pants legs when we see such a truckload of manure coming our way? The riot was the *exact opposite* of what the GOP leaders try to claim, although, truth be told, there is nothing new in such semantic deception. Is this not always the way of a political party rushing headlong to the Right until it finds out that it has nowhere else to go and must adopt blatantly dishonest tactics and policies? Lies and euphemisms multiply and pile high upon themselves, one dishonest phrase begetting another.

Fact: Trump extremists committed inexcusable riotous and insurrectionary acts on January 6th, acts that shocked the whole nation. GOP apologists then argued that it was actually "something else" as though a violent riot had not taken place at all! They dared take visible truth and attempted to twist it into its opposite. *No riot or insurrection is ever lawful or legitimate (the GOP leaders should know as much) but they bury their heads in the sand and choose to pretend otherwise.*

68

The events of that day proved beyond a shadow of a doubt that what has been missing from the GOP for far too long is "legitimate political discourse," if they intend to excuse such violent insurrectionary acts. They obviously have lost all sense of the true meaning and purpose of America's Constitution if they are willing to engage in such cheap sophistry bolstered by outright lies. The moderates have lost their voices in a bout of cowardice if they do nothing while extremists seize control of their party.

If any Republicans dare criticize Trump or work with Democrats to pass legislation or further a congressional investigation, they are treated as outcasts. The constant Republican refusal of collaboration across the aisle has become a standard tactic and is now more typical than the exception. Instead, Trump and his followers pridefully preen themselves on having given the nation the spectacle of riot and disorder, of mayhem and destruction. The Trumpistas have long thrived on creating fear and division in the country through chicanery and deception. Their abandonment of principles of the U.S. Constitution is clear and unmistakable; they are turning their backs on over two hundred years of constitutional law and ethics. Many supporters blindly followed Trump in his ill-conceived and *illegitimate* attempt to steal a presidential election! That is a corrupting influence that should never be seen coming from the White House.

A citizen who does not understand the fundamental importance of candidates being elected fairly and openly by majority vote cannot be counted on to support America's democratic institutions and values. Anyone who thinks it is "legitimate" for a candidate to lie and cheat to acquire power doesn't understand the first thing about American democracy. Any political party that believes it is engaging in "legitimate discourse" when a Trump-inspired mob explodes into riot and insurrection, doesn't grasp that we are a nation of laws. Integrity is expected of elected officials, including the president: especially the president. It is simply *not* legitimate to engage in riot and insurrection to advance one's personal goals. It is *not* legitimate to commit crimes to overturn an election!

In the here and now, law enforcement agencies have begun prosecuting rioters who broke numerous laws in their vain attempt to stop the results of a fair and free election from being affirmed. Many felonies were committed that day; hundreds of violence-prone insurrectionists have been arrested and are being prosecuted and convicted, with more sure to follow. The longer sentences will be measured not in months but in years. Jail sentences of as much as ten and twenty years indicate the seriousness with which judges and juries are taking these charges; a large number of insurrectionists are jailhouse bound. Whether their Trump-worshiping ideology remains intact a decade or two from now, remains to be seen.

All that being known, it is shocking to see GOP leaders trying to conjure up a pleasant-sounding euphemism for that awful day. They wish to see how many Americans are naïve enough to accept the insurrection of January 6th represented as "legitimate political discourse". What shall we be persuaded to accept next: a riot being called a "legitimate peaceful picnic"?

Trump's divisive effect on the nation and its people has taken a turn for the worst. "Trumpism" has now been extended to include a well-planned attack on the seat of government itself and, indirectly, an unwarranted assault on the English language, where words and concepts are twisted into unrecognizable forms. Rightwingers are trying to present a hate-filled society as the American norm when it's not; if this curiously illegitimate three-word phrase is taken seriously, then there is no rhyme or reason to life.

As for "political": what has this word always conveyed in American history?

- It means the War of Independence and the American Revolution.
- It means the Declaration of Independence.
- It means the Constitution of the United States.
- It means the people's right to self-government and individual liberties guaranteed under law.
- It means the right of the American people to engage in the free expression of ideas and to vote for

candidates who they believe will best represent their needs and the needs of the country.

- It means elections are conducted by secret ballot and decided by majority vote.

The phrase "legitimate political discourse" may be useful in some other context but it can *never* include actual riot and insurrection. Any person familiar with American history and who treasures democratic principles, will not fall for this ludicrous attempt at substituting a phony euphemism for the violent vandalism and criminal assaults that occurred during those horrendous and unspeakable hours of a riotous afternoon on January 6, 2021. The Republican Party's feeble efforts to justify or excuse such an insurrection shows the GOP is no longer behaving like a legitimate political party but has fallen under the hypnotic sway of rightwing extremists, led by a twice-impeached narcissist willing to do and say anything to keep himself in power, or regain it once lost. That includes inciting a riot in the nation's capital; he may have tried to keep at arm's length his most ardent followers who staged these violent acts of riot and insurrection *but it was all done in his name and at his beck and call.*

During the backlash of revulsion that swept across the nation, he began to distance himself from the violent actions of that day but his lack of meaningful action on January 6th speaks volumes. His name will be associated with the riotous insurrection in every history textbook for decades. The "person" and the "riot" have become inseparable, entwined to such a degree that only an ignoramus or a madman could fail to see the connection. Yet, at present, various GOP leaders still seem incapable of engaging in reasonable political discourse. They seem unable to admit openly what happened that day; they are afraid to repudiate it and to place blame where it must fall: on the rioters and the one man who incited them to riot. There was nothing remotely resembling "reasonable discourse" in what happened that day; *there was nothing lawful or "legitimate" about that terrifying riot that threatened the lives of police officers and elected representatives convened to carry out their constitutional duty.*

Trump's insurrection endangered our system of free elections; it threatened one of the bedrock principles of American freedom and justice. He and his loyalists behaved no differently than a mob trying to overthrow an elected government through the use of force and violence. A new truth stands exposed; the rightwing of the Republican Party appears committed to opposing America's constitutional democracy in subtle and nefarious ways if given half the chance. The American people must remain aware and on guard; the extremists will try worse tactics when and if the opportunity presents itself.

Trump bides his time in Mar-a-Lago while his narcissism dreams of regaining power, even if it can only be accomplished by overthrowing the results of a free and fair election. He has arrived at the fail-safe boundary; rather than conceding he lost the election, he is attempting to pierce the boundary's historical steadfastness in a vain attempt to regain power "by any means necessary." It is no coincidence that such thinking typically describes the beliefs and actions of authoritarian figures, of dictators and tyrants throughout history, men willing to toss aside all standards of ethical and lawful behavior for momentary gain and now a Republican ex-president has joined them.

The GOP must measure carefully how well these shameful tricks and strategies will play with the American people, come the midterm elections at the end of the year. For voters who have had their eyes opened by January 6th, such a man as Trump cannot be considered a comrade to the Founding Fathers. He is not a soul-mate to Jefferson; he is not a disciple of Adams or Madison; he is not a peer of Franklin or Paine. Quite the contrary: Trump has thrown in his lot with the nation's rightwing forces opposed to American democracy; he appears intent on undermining traditional democratic principles and procedures wherever it suits his purpose.

He did not willingly accept constitutional limits on himself; the first tell-tale sign of tyrannical thinking occurs when a leader thinks he is "above the law." In place of conscience and adherence to the law, Trump was tempted to seize power by violating an election and declaring himself president (as he tried to do). Even Trump in the fullness of his conceit must know he cannot get away with an outright seizure of power. That does not mean the topic is off the table but a "putsch" is for the time being too impractical and alarming to the American people. Regaining power by stealth and subterfuge becomes his alternative strategy.

The clumsy and transparent foolishness of the phrase "legitimate political discourse" to describe a *violent insurrection* is worrisome enough but we must also consider it a harbinger of worse deceits yet to come. The GOP leaders are becoming all too adept at these lies of hypocrisy; perhaps in their eyes an unabashed liar like Trump is heaven-sent and that is why they are not done with him. Still, that they attempt to offer such a whitewashed phrase to describe the events of January 6 at this late date is indicative of their determination to regain power, whatever the cost. Among his most extreme supporters, they have convinced themselves, through ignorance, reactionary inflexibility and cult-like intransigence, that....

- Trump didn't lose the popular vote.
- The courts didn't throw out over sixty challenges as unwarranted and unsubstantiated.
- Trump didn't lose in the Electoral College by a landslide 306 to 232.
- Trump didn't incite his base to riot.
- Trump didn't applaud, condone, encourage, and support violent insurrectionists.
- The widespread turmoil and violence of that day was only an example of so-called "legitimate political discourse."

Do the Republicans expect us to take such deceitful foolishness seriously?

Let the trials continue!

Let Lady Justice speak!!

****

Tracking Trump

"And if it requires pardons, we will give them pardons, because they are being treated so unfairly." (Jan. 2021)

I spent over five years of my life studying Trump and warning, in writing, of the acute danger he presents to our constitutional democracy. His latest miscue, however, has barely gotten a rise out of me. I am referring to his remarks about how if he became president in 2024 he would consider issuing pardons for the January 6th insurrectionists. Isn't that shocking? Consider the damage done: "According to a May 2021 estimate by the Architect of the Capitol, the attack caused approximately $1.5 million worth of damage to the U.S. Capitol building."[14] That was in May 2021 but by April 2022 the estimate had increased significantly: "Capitol Riot Costs Go Up: Government Estimates $2.73 Million In Property Damage"[15]

Over 700 rioters were arrested, eleven for seditious conspiracy, and the trials are far from over.

---

[14]https://www.justice.gov/usao-dc/one-year-jan-6-attack-capitol (retrieved on 11/25/22)

[15]https://www.forbes.com/sites/zacharysmith/2022/04/08/capitol-riot-costs-go-up-government-estimates-273-million-in-property-damage/ (retrieved on 11/25/22).

Yet Trump would look kindly upon those felonious lawbreakers who attacked the Capitol Building to stop Congress from doing its duty; the rioters damaged and destroyed millions of dollars of property and injured 114 police officers. Just like an out-of-control mob they ran amuck, hunting down elected representatives to confront, harangue, and possibly harm. Nancy Pelosi, Speaker of the House, and Vice-President Mike Pence were both high up on the list of "traitors" they wished to punish.

This was the first major attack by right-wing domestic terrorists aimed directly against the United States government. The man who made all this possible was none other than the soon-to-be ex-president himself, Donald J. Trump. Yes, a president of the United States inspired his supporters to attack the Capitol: to physically invade America's hitherto sacrosanct halls of democratic government. Among the mob were men threatening to injure or kill prominent Democratic congressmen in order to stop Congress from verifying the results of a free election!

Donald Trump is proving himself to be an even greater danger to American democracy than his strongest critics previously thought possible. He has started spreading the Big Lie, believing he would always have followers loyal enough to act upon anything he said, no matter how false, no matter how improbable. So you see, that's why it's hard for me to get riled up by his latest statement about pardoning the rioters if given half a chance. It is a bridge the American people will cross when and if such circumstances arise, which remains problematic. He was not re-elected in 2020 which shows that a majority of Americans already rejected him once and appear more than capable of defeating him again.

His "possibility-of-pardon" statement suggests that he recognizes his riotous supporters stand a good chance of being convicted; after all, you needn't worry about pardoning an innocent person who has broken no law. Trump and his followers don't usually bother to reason things out that way; no doubt some of Donald's most provocative statements are designed for his base and not necessarily the legal system or the nation as a whole. Trump occupies a peculiar position in politics parallel to that of a cult leader in religion; therefore, he can dangle the promise of a pardon as catnip for his loyalists with no discussion of specific crimes or the names of protestors facing trial or already convicted.

Would he pardon a felony as well as a misdemeanor? How many would he pardon? He fails to say. For Trump, that could mean one rioter or it could mean a hundred: who knows? And what possible reason would he give for such a pardon? Is it because he wishes to claim the arrested rioters didn't do what they were caught on video doing *in flagrante delicto*?[16] Or perhaps he wishes to say what they did was "right" and so he must set them free? What exceptional circumstances or appeal for mercy could he cite? What political theory would move him to consider pardoning

---

[16] In the very act of committing the offense; in other words, caught red-handed.

the violent insurrectionists who attacked the Capitol? Would he claim that they rioted for *him* as though he had won the presidency, even though he didn't?

He was a lame-duck by that time, the period between November's election and January's inauguration. That's when the outgoing president usually does little or nothing in terms of proposing legislation, even though the oath has yet to be administered to his successor: in this case, Joe Biden. Does Trump man up and gracefully accept his loss to keep intact the American tradition of a peaceful transition of power? Not Trump! What does he offer as his parting gift to the country? *He inspires a riotous insurrection and then suggests he might pardon them*!

He has been dog-whistling not just conservative Republicans but extreme right-wingers; his words encouraged his followers to march to the Capitol, including groups with a known penchant for violence, such as the Proud Boys and the Oath Keepers, the latter a far-right anti-government militia. In countries wherever fascism got a toehold, provoking civil disturbances by "stirring things up" was a regular hallmark of fascist tactics. Trump's "promise" to consider pardoning the rioters may have had an additional personal motive, since he no doubt hoped to convince arrested rioters to keep their mouths shut; some of them might know details of when and where the actual planning for the attack took place, which could further implicate Trump and his associates.

He had already set a precedent with Roger Stone when he pardoned a "loyalist" convicted of seven crimes, including obstruction, false statements, and witness tampering. In February 2020, Roger Stone was sentenced to forty months or over three years in prison. If one reviews the televised images, Roger Stone remained remarkably cocky all during his arrest, trial, and conviction. How does a man, soon-to-be a convicted felon, remain so flamboyantly optimistic? How does Roger Stone smile and make jokes right after being sentenced to prison? In a short while (July 2020) he received a pardon from Trump and walked free; there we had our answer. In the *New York Times* of Jan. 26, 2021 an article states:

"In his final hours as president, Donald J. Trump doled out pardons and commutations to dozens of people, including supporters, political figures, rappers and defendants in high-profile criminal cases....The announcements came nearly a month after Mr. Trump pardoned, among others, Charles Kushner, the father of his son-in-law and senior adviser, Jared Kushner; Paul Manafort, his 2016 campaign chairman; and Roger J. Stone Jr., his longtime informal adviser and friend whose sentence the president had commuted in July."[17]

For whom did Trump aim these words, that he would consider pardoning the rioters? Who would be glad to see the insurrectionists go free if not those very same individuals and organizations who acted and believed most like them, including other rightwingers, white

---

[17]https://www.nytimes.com/article/who-did-trump-pardon.html (retrieved on 11/25/22). He also pardoned Steve Bannon, Anthony Levandowski and Lil Wayne.

supremacists, and domestic terrorists? Only a man with a grandiose vision of overturning an election would conclude he should be allowed to do whatever he wishes: even pardon lawfully-convicted rioters who attempted an insurrection in the nation's capital city, the heart of American democracy!

It is exactly how power-hungry figures try to tighten their grip on the reins of government while weakening the checks-and-balances system distributed through all three branches. Trump plays footsies with questionable tactics and convinces himself that everybody loves him but that ship has sailed. Many Americans have now seen a side of Trump that not all knew was there. The pundits and history books will have to decide, when assessing his presidency, whether he was merely mediocre and narcissistic, a selfish greedy bumbler, or the first in a line of devious men aiming to dramatically increase presidential power and authority over American citizens.

Look at the history of Adolf Hitler and the Nazis in Germany. He appointed a minister of propaganda who was shockingly brazen in his lies and deceits. The Nazis promulgated the notion the bigger the lie, the more easily it is believed. It was a strangely bizarre tactic but the Nazis made full use of it. Hitler believed he could convince the German people to believe anything they were told, including the "fact" that they were descended from a mythical Aryan race destined to rule the world.

He engaged in psychosis-tinged tirades: the Jews are to blame! Attack and kill the Jews! Hitler learned to magnify his own anti-Semitic feelings until it mushroomed into a messianic crusade which turned into the "Final Solution": nothing less than a demand for the genocidal extinction of all Jews everywhere. Hitler got halfway to his goal of genocide and the conquest of Europe but in the East the Russians proved surprisingly stubborn and intractable.

Nor could the Underground Resistance in conquered countries be stopped. The Red Army fought valiantly until the Allies opened a Second Front in 1944, catching Hitler in the grip of an iron vice that would squeeze him and Nazism to death. Today's generation of would-be fascist followers of a Fuehrer (or an authoritarian figure of some kind) tend to forget how that history turned out, don't they? In the end, the fascists were crushed. Germany was in shambles, many of her cities destroyed.[18] Hitler was in a panic trying to arrange for his own suicide with the additional proviso that his body be burned so the Allies could not recognize him.

Such an attempt was made but not successfully; the dead, partially-charred body of Adolf Hitler was found and identified. Thus did the Third Reich come to an abrupt end. And yet that remains one of the fantasy illusions of the Far Right in America: that they will find

---

[18] "During the Second World War, Allied air forces dropped nearly two million tons of bombs on Germany, destroying some 60 cities..." (retrieved on 11/25/22) https://politics.utoronto.ca/publication/fire-and-fury-the -allied-bombing-of-germany-1942-1945

a leader they can follow, a strong man like Hitler who can impose his will on them and the nation. If not an outright dictator, then a strong president willing to tolerate or support their rightwing beliefs with policies that will benefit the wealthy, preserve the status quo, and protect white supremacists.

Looking back, Hitler must have been one hell of a cocky fuehrer; he thought he could defeat Russia in six weeks and then turn his attention to unconquered countries in Western Europe at his leisure, his armies still at full strength. The World War I corporal miscalculated but the neo-Nazis in America still think of him as an archetypal kind of leader. Racists in America dream of a leader in the White House who will be an unapologetic white supremacist, ready to change things along racial lines and ensure that the white race always ends up on top. (The white racists and domestic terrorists most prone to violence will be locked up as felons long before anything like that ever happens.)

Nevertheless, in the racist's eyes, Trump holds out hope that somehow he'll find a way to make America "white" again. They got this far, perhaps they can get even farther! It's not going to happen but Trump knows how to play their game; he is good at stringing people along and pretending that he can make their wishes come true. Self-delusion and deluding others happens to be one of his strengths; he knows how to turn empty promises into cash.

As for how the war turned out for the maniac Adolf Hitler? The Russians poured in from the east along a hundred mile front, covering twenty miles or more per day as they drove the Nazis out of Russia and headed straight for Berlin, revenge-minded and unstoppable. In the west D-Day arrived; on June 6, 1944 more than 160,000 Allied soldiers stormed the beaches of Normandy and began their fierce push inland. The U.S., England, France, Canada, Australia, the Netherlands, Belgium, Norway, Greece, and Yugoslavia combined forces and began pushing forward with men and machines.

Hitler had his hands full; he began giving unrealistic orders to his generals that they knew were impossible to carry out. They were under attack from both east and west while facing constant harassment and acts of sabotage from anti-Nazi partisans. The heroic stories of the resistance movement in countries such as France and Yugoslavia are so remarkable they form their own chapter and can move one to tears; the partisans' never-say-die attitude include many tales of bravery and sacrifice as noteworthy as those acts of valor performed by soldiers during bloody battles where large armies clashed and fought for supremacy.

All of us can learn something from studying World War II and how the freedom-loving peoples of the world came together to crush fascism. Unfortunately, when Trump studied World War II, he learned the wrong kind of lesson. He saw that prejudice is a long-lived creature that can easily be inflamed anew. He didn't focus on the courage and sacrifice of ordinary soldiers who made that Allied victory possible: not in the least. No, he's thinking that if the

January 6th rioters get convicted, he might be able to get people to vote for him if he promises to consider issuing pardons for the insurrectionists if they are treated unfairly. "Unfairly" apparently means conviction in an open court of law where the highest standards of evidence are maintained in the search for facts and truth as the day of reckoning draws near.

For Trump and the way he thinks, his offer probably makes sense. He already pardoned Roger Stone, a convicted felon, and others: why not rioting insurrectionists who threatened American democracy? Why draw the line anywhere? Why not pardon violent individuals who attempted to prevent the results of a free election from being verified? Trump looks for the levers of Machiavellian power, not the scales of Jeffersonian morality and justice.

In any event, there have been so many stupefying statements by Trump over the years that even his latest utterance doesn't get this author all that worked up any longer. There are good reasons for my upbeat mood: for one thing, he's no longer president. That's something to celebrate! The truth is, Trump can no longer abuse the authority of the office because, whether he's ready to admit it or not, he's no longer president. No more Trump nepotism, no more favors for cronies, no more pardons for convicted felons like Roger Stone.

Of course, no one thinks that the long-term political fight is over but it's nice to get a break from his unpredictability, at least for a little while. Yes, we all know he continuously prevaricates and utters barbs to get under people's skin. Yes, we know he employs all kinds of tricks to ensure his base will stay with him; however, this author also believes a growing number of Americans have come to realize he's not quite normal or sensible, not in the way they have viewed other presidents and statesmen. His fiercest critics take it one step farther; they think he's unstable and responsible for increasing hate, division, and violence in this country, including how he sparked the January 6th riot in Washington, D.C.

Every week the House Committee is making progress in finding out what really happened on January 6th and who the key players were, including his loyalist rightwing extremists. It would be naive to think Trump and his buddies had no hand in the doings of the day; a thorough investigation may turn up some of the missing connections between anti-government militias, white supremacists and persons near or within Trump's inner circle. The Committee's report will likely include a scathing indictment of the role Trump played in inciting what was clearly a *planned* riot. Ultimately, he alone must be held responsible for the violent insurrection!

****

In Other News

Trump is under pressure from numerous investigations and lawsuits, including possible prosecutions in Georgia and New York involving electoral interference and questions concerning his unethical and/or law-breaking behavior, predictably on the financial side. In his four years in office, his most notable "success" was figuring out how to divide and polarize the American people. His major effect on the country was to create division and strife. Indeed, he proved rather expert in dividing Americans against one another; he made an uncommon word like "divisiveness" part of our daily vocabulary.

Some people have a knack for making a mess and profiting from it; Trump fits the profile perfectly. To paraphrase a sentiment from H.L. Mencken, nobody ever lost money *underestimating* the intelligence of the American people and it seems some politicians have a knack for exploiting such a situation. Could it be true? A group of Americans would have to be pretty dumb to deserve an insult like that. Where could we ever find such a group? I know! Maybe people who vote for a candidate of whom it may rightly be said he was impeached not once but *twice* by the House. Even ten Senators of his own party voted to convict him in 2021 (joining Senator Mitt Romney, the only Republican who voted to convict him in 2019 for being "guilty of an appalling abuse of public trust".) The pattern is clear, however; the number of Senators voting to impeach are ascending.

Trump believes he can escape from any situation; even so, the number is growing of journalists and scholars who believe he is in over his head and in considerable legal jeopardy. One doesn't have to be anti-Trump to see how serious the legal charges are. At times, his brash "you-can't-touch-me!" attitude reminds one of the post-Civil War era of "the Robber Barons." The name refers to the richest men in the country who plundered resources, monopolized industries, and profited handsomely from pursuing their goals with ruthless determination. They were incredibly ambitious and greed-driven; they did whatever was necessary to multiply their millions of dollars.

They showed few moral scruples in getting what they desired by hook or by crook. Trump would fit right in with men like John D. Rockefeller, Andre Carnegie, Cornelius Vanderbilt, Jay Gould, and others of that class. They were far too rich and powerful to be opposed or restrained by just anyone; they barged forward in any direction they wished, each in his own unique way. Of course, many substantial legal reforms have occurred since the long-ago Era of Robber Barons. Today, our nation's national and international reputation depends in large part on its laws being enforced, ethical standards being set and followed, and elected leaders demonstrating they are not open to bribery or financial chicanery. In America, both businessmen and politicians should not be tempted by get-rich-quick schemes when such stratagems involve unethical and illegal conduct.

Scandals continue to occur from time to time but they are less frequent than formerly, perhaps more the exception than the rule. One can well imagine how these more stringent ethical standards of the last several decades must chafe the skin of those men and women who would like to increase their wealth at a faster pace; the policy of "deregulation" usually has at least a whiff of this self-aggrandizement tendency. For a time, limits were placed on campaign donations to help level the playing field among candidates but the Supreme Court's decision in *Citizens United v. Federal Election Commission* (2010) put a halt to most of those efforts.

As a consequence, there is now less oversight of the richest individuals and families, businesses and corporations that provide much of the dark money to fund the right-wing of the Republican Party and its current leaders. Until recently, it remained an open question among certain millionaires and billionaires whether they were getting enough "bang for the buck." Perhaps they weren't, at least not until the ascendancy of Trump to the presidency in 2016: here comes their promised tax cut!

Trump's motto seemed to be: Step Right Up and Grab the Money, All You Rich People: it's ours now! Let's unite political-and-economic-control in one person: ME! How embarrassing it must be for him to see how his reputation keeps getting ruined by interruptions like impeachment proceedings and court cases. Those constitutional and legal processes overseeing his wayward behavior kind of threw a monkey wrench into the whole works, didn't it?

Then the Trump Ego hit upon a new solution: denial and lies! His phone call to Zelensky was "perfect;" in truth, he abused the office of the presidency by threatening President Zelensky to withhold aid from Ukraine unless Zelensky helped dig up dirt on Trump's opponent. That brought on Trump's first impeachment; by the time of the second trial just one year later, it was for *fomenting an insurrection.* His unruly behavior and awful decision-making worsened rapidly in late 2020. He had nowhere else to go so he felt compelled to deny Joe Biden won the election: "Lie, lie, lie!" In his head he must be holding an imaginary conversation that goes something like this:

"The Democrats cheated by stuffing the voting box. Can I prove it? You have some nerve asking me that! You know I have no proof. Over sixty courts have thrown out all my challenges. Doesn't that answer your question? No, I can't prove *any* of the allegations. Who cares? I am keeping my base together and they are sending me lots of money! Guess what, I'm STILL the president! There are people who want me to be president, who believe I *am* the president. Okay, they threw me out of the White House but I'll be back. I'm Donald the Great! I can do anything!"

Yes, he threw a temper tantrum of humongous magnitude after the 2020 election but when a man controls the flow of millions of dollars the way he can, then even a hissy fit has hidden purpose. Trump has cash to spare to mislead his followers through false claims and artful smearing of his opponents. For that reason, the right-wing threat must always be taken seriously; their ethical boundaries are dangerously unstable. It is a particular feature of authoritarianism, of fascism, that no matter how often the statements of a rising faction become glaringly false and contradictory, the members of that faction never concede they made a mistake; *they cannot and will not admit they could be wrong.* This is true even when their statements are full of factual blunders and irrational stupidities, obvious and plain for all to see. That's a form of intellectual intolerance and intransigence of the worst kind, now regularly practiced by Trump and the GOP.

A racist cannot admit that a black person is his equal; an anti-Semite cannot admit Jewish persons are normal human beings; a male chauvinist cannot believe women should be as well-educated as a man or play a larger leadership role in an organization than men; the male chauvinist does not believe a woman should enjoy the same rights and freedoms he has. In the same way, a fascist cannot endure the thought that individuals prefer liberty in a democracy rather than the oppressive stamp of the iron boot of a ruthless dictator.

When any group on the American political spectrum begins to believe it is infallible, trouble will surely follow. It is a normal and regular part of growing up, of reaching adult maturity, for a human being to recognize and admit a mistake. The GOP, on the other hand, is populated with extremists who say absurd things for which they never apologize, unless the false statement provokes such an up-swelling of public outcry that some kind of rationalized retraction becomes unavoidable.

These days, certain Republicans seem to enjoy making ridiculous statements rife with contradictions and falsehoods, led by Trump setting the most outrageous examples. The "say anything" apologists and provocateurs like to sow confusion and skepticism wherever they can, including setting in motion loops of outrageous conspiracy theories through social media. Indeed, they appear to celebrate this ploy as one of their most successful political stratagems; no matter how dangerous and ill-advised the claim, they never seem willing to abandon or disown their baseless accusations as long as it creates a stir somewhere.

Trump's dependence on "half-truths" is another way in which the Republican Party is moving away from traditional expectations of honest conduct in the White House. A president need not dumb down to the American people; he need not assume the American people can't handle the truth. Trump's particular form of political dishonesty reflects his tendency to believe that many Americans can be fooled into believing anything. Besides refusing to admit their errors and misstatement of facts, the leaders of the Republican Party display their intransigence and inflexibility in another way. The GOP leaders frequently refuse to work in a bipartisan manner, thereby failing to respond to the needs of their constituencies except along the narrowest partisan lines. By subtle words and crass deeds, they are leading their most enthusiastic followers toward doubting the viability of democracy itself. The promotion of such hypocrisy and skepticism is becoming a way of life for Republican extremists; they are leaving the door open for fascism to gain a toehold.

In the past, a journalist catching a politician behaving "hypocritically," saying one thing but doing another, was considered akin to the kiss of death. If the press got hold of a candidate contradicting himself from one speech to the next, critics had a field day. If a candidate got caught fudging the truth or making irreconcilable promises to different groups on different days, that was super-fodder for the opposition to pursue and vanquish! Today, the current GOP doesn't seem to care about the accusation of "hypocrisy" when it is leveled at them, as though depending on contradictory statements and transparent falsehoods no longer counts as a moral lapse. The top Republicans willingly engage in misleading statements and artful deception; what becomes even more striking and worrisome is the fact they no longer try to hide such hypocrisy.

It is another fascist-like tendency; tell a whopper and swear to stand by it forever! The Big Lie remains essentially a fascist-like tactic and yet they will not concede as much directly. As for anyone naively expecting an apology for such hypocrisy and false statements, it appears that ship has sailed. Trump didn't win the 2020 election but how many GOP leaders are willing to say so aloud? In the meanwhile, the GOP's time-honored claim that it is the party of "law and order" is becoming a national joke. Leaving aside for a moment the usual clash of wills on Capitol Hill, Trump's rioters in Washington D.C. showed they weren't capable of respecting the basic concept of "law and order" when they themselves became the egregious law-breakers aiming to disrupt Congressional certification of an election and peaceful transition of power. The MAGA rioters became the party of "lawlessness and disorder" so gross and unprovoked was their attack on the Capitol Building and Congress.

The badly-deceived rioters committed a host of horrific crimes that day. Their out-of-control behavior was so shocking that even a (frightened) Republican leader or two urged the president to take action to *calm the crowd*. Several of the GOP leaders, out of fear for their own safety (mobs can be very unpredictable) rebuked Trump. Later, they would attempt to return to a nonchalant attitude of "business as usual" but the intensity of their initial panic speaks volumes regarding the horrors that everyone witnessed that day.

This was a crisis of historic proportions suddenly thrust upon the nation, so much so that even a few of the most stalwart Republicans became genuinely concerned that the dangerous riot might spin out of control. They knew that Trump had his hand in it and so they appealed to him to urge his supporters to stop the violence. He refused to accede to their requests for *over three hours*. For these leaders, there was such an instinctive response to seeing their nation's capital

95

under siege that they couldn't help but react with shock and outrage. Trump, according to all accounts, watched the television reports and appeared to enjoy what he was seeing.

However, this temporary willingness to utter words of condemnation faded so fast that you practically needed a stop-watch to time it; you had to watch the news in slow motion in order to catch a glimpse of it at all. Most of the Republicans reversed course within a day or two and quickly fell in lock-step behind Trump's ever-present narcissistic and disingenuous habits. Yes, the top GOP leaders failed to condemn *an insurrectionary attack* in a consistent and forthright manner, even though they knew the rioters were engaged in a violent attempt to stop Congress from certifying the results of a free election. It was treasonous and yet they quieted out of fear of *him*.

Always thus: when a Big Lie is allowed to gain traction in any political arena, outright violence is never far behind. Loyalists in Trump's base launched a direct assault on American democracy with mayhem, injury and death. To this day, many of the rioters still support the one man who inspired this violence aimed at overturning the results of a presidential election. Trump's "cult of the personality" remains a phenomenon unto itself but the horrifying events of January 6th told the nation that something was going on that went far beyond personal traits and partisan political differences; the nation's democratic form of government was itself at stake!

The rioters were finally dispersed but one shudders to think what might have happened if the insurrectionists had gotten their hands on Nancy Pelosi or Mike Pence. Mob psychology can develop a terrifying momentum of its own, one violent deed leading to a worse one. Meanwhile, Trump sat and did nothing for hours despite the oath he took to "preserve, protect and defend the Constitution of the United States." He was obliged to fulfill his oath and yet, instead, he became the leader of the faction that *threatened* both Congress and the Constitution. His followers attacked the government that Trump had sworn an oath to defend and protect. Instead, he became their leader and chief instigator of the trouble that was to ensue.

Think of the chaos and confusion Trump brought to the results of an election, actions based on a lie and wholly unnecessary. All any losing candidate has to do is to be gracious and conciliatory in defeat by acknowledging the outcome; he is expected to wish his victorious opponent well and to take part in the social protocols involved in a peaceful transfer of power. But Trump couldn't even do that much; he couldn't behave like a regular human being. The warning signs had been present for the previous four years; Trump demonstrated repeatedly that he did not have it in his character to behave in a calm, reasonable, and responsible way even when such presidential behavior was most needed. At the end of his term, he would sooner fire up a mob of rioters than simply acknowledge his loss; he would sooner edge the country toward greater polarization, with an increasing potential for violence, than accept defeat. That, too, is a clear and unmistakable Trump trait; it is a clear and unmistakable trait of authoritarian leaders as well.

The Republican Party has always insisted it would protect the American people from any enemy trying to hurt America, yet members of that party willingly engaged in the very behavior about which the GOP once warned. The Republican Party will protect America from all enemies, foreign and domestic, they loudly proclaimed, an assertion whose validity appears to be slipping away year by year. Members of *their* party have traduced the very meaning of law and order; they have engaged in riotous acts of domestic terrorism on a grand scale when they attacked the Capitol; the insurrectionists tried to intimidate Congress into surrendering the government to a mob when the results of a free election rejected their candidate in no uncertain terms. In doing so, Trump loyalists abandoned defending the sanctity of American elections, the very heart of our nation's freedom. Trump's big lie set the events of that day in motion; he alone bears ultimate responsibility for the mob's attempt to overthrow democracy.

If that is how the GOP intends to "protect" our constitutional democracy, by riot and insurrection, one would be safe to surmise they are now only offering platitudes and empty promises rather than honorable principles. Whatever the GOP leaders stated in the past about protecting America, they do not appear serious about doing so any longer; they are less the defenders and more the protagonists seeking to undermine America's constitutional democracy.

Trump has developed his cult-of-the-personality much farther than anyone else. It is hard for many Republicans to accept the fact that their party leader, Donald Trump, poses a danger to our constitutional republic, a danger greater than that posed by any other individual. No doubt the followers of Jim Jones believed in him, too; they could not see that following him blindly would lead to an unmitigated disaster in Guyana with over 900 men, women, and children dead from suicide and murder. Once cult members get hooked a certain way, it is exceedingly difficult for them to free themselves from their delusions or for anyone else to offer advice or warning. The cult leader in religion or politics typically has a special kind of charisma which his followers mistake for leadership; he often displays an unrepentant arrogance which followers mistake for confidence and certainty.

Initially, the cult leader and followers agree on certain issues and that's all that matters; after that, his supporters seem unable to analyze situations rationally as they develop a "blind loyalty". They can no longer tolerate disagreement with whatever their cult leader is advocating. Taken in that context, the gap between the followers of Jim Jones and Donald Trump is not as big as it might first appear. Supporters of a cult-like leader, whether religious or political, move rapidly toward a position of extreme intransigence where their opinions are no longer part of a fair-minded exchange; they and they alone are always right. The GOP could not maintain a moderate position and beat the Democrats consistently so they took the plunge to the Far Right. They are, in effect, preparing ways to use deceit and violence in contradistinction to over two hundred years of a peaceful electoral process and reputable transition.

Some pundits may be shy to say so but the GOP leaders are behaving more like the British king's Loyalists than Patriots at the time of the American Revolution: that is, they are constantly taking the most conservative "status quo" position available and showing a marked willingness to sacrifice or suppress civil liberties for some groups of Americans, usually minorities. The American Revolution stood for an expansion of human rights; today's GOP stands for its contraction.

Ironically, the Republican Party of Lincoln's time was anti-slavery and radical but the modern GOP has abandoned that historic legacy. Indeed, they have flipped their position entirely in order to become the more conservative of the two major parties. The GOP leaders appear to feel no embarrassment or shame for their party's evolution into the exact opposite of what it once was. The Republicans after the Civil War kept progressive planks in their platform until the 1920's, when business interests became the dominant concern and more important than protecting civil rights.

By the 1930's the Republicans were becoming reactionary and more interested in defending the interests of the wealthiest class than addressing the needs of working people, while millions of unemployed Americans suffered from hunger and inadequate income. The GOP under Hoover did little to alleviate the suffering of their countrymen. They had adopted the notion of "laissez faire" and letting local communities and charities handle the crisis.[19] Only the threat of social upheaval and revolution made them keep quiet and bide their time; after the anti-fascist war was over, the Republican Party re-emerged and again adopted the most conservative policies, including efforts to undo important planks of FDR's New Deal. They became openly anti-union and neglected or opposed popular movements for racial justice. Even today, the GOP appears to be looking for ways to get rid of the safety net; there is talk of "privatizing" Social Security (no doubt to the benefit of a few and the detriment of millions of others).

Whenever a political party announces planks in its official platform, discerning readers must distinguish between empty promises and realizable action plans. The Republicans don't bother to monitor themselves as they become the opposite of what they once claimed to be. They promote themselves as the conservative party of law and order and yet tolerate an insurrection in the nation's capital. They want Americans to trust them but how can anyone forget that it was Trump's MAGA

---

[19] Laissez faire: a policy or attitude of letting events take their own course without interference; in economics, it means abstention by governments from interfering in the workings of the free market.

supporters who smashed windows and doors to unlawfully occupy the Capitol while shouting they wanted to hang Vice-President Mike Pence?

Recently, a leader of the Proud Boys, Jeremy Bertino, pled guilty to *seditious conspiracy*, as have four members of the Oath Keepers. Bertino has agreed to cooperate with prosecutors in building their case against other leaders of the Proud Boys, some of whom have ties with Roger Stone and Alex Jones, outspoken supporters of Donald Trump. Clearly, the right-wing of the Republican Party was involved in the push to overturn the election. This insurrectionary riot is one of the sure signs by which the American people can tell whether a political party is moving toward defending American democracy or away from it. Expanding voter rights is *democratic*; pushing through gerrymandered districts and voter-suppression laws is *undemocratic*.

This approach is based on the Constitution's view that all citizens over the age of eighteen have the right to vote.[20] Refusing to accept the results of an election is anti-democratic in the extreme; it is as far from the vision of the Founding Fathers as one could possibly imagine. It is not in keeping with the concept of self-government for GOP-controlled state legislatures *to make it harder for citizens to vote*. They do so by engaging in partisan gerrymandering, purging voter rolls, reducing the number of polling places, shortening the window of time for voting, and making it

---

[20] See the fifteenth, nineteenth, and twenty-sixth Amendments for more details.

more difficult to vote by employing a multitude of other strategies. It is, in essence, a form of cheating: nothing less, nothing more.

The GOP is engaged in state-by-state campaigns to control the outcome of future elections through gerrymandering and voter suppression laws. They do much of their manipulations in the open and remain unapologetic for attempting to affect election results in this manner. That's not "conservative" Republicanism; that's cheating, that's stealing, that's anti-democratic, and that's incipient fascism.

Yes, Trump's latest statements about pardoning the rioters are aggravating but they are not quite as worrisome as they once were. Normal, reasonable people have had a chance to observe him for four years and to take careful measure of the man. The House Committee is investigating what happened on January 6; he is also facing numerous legal actions to hold him accountable for other alleged misdeeds. In a democracy, such legal processes necessarily take time to ensure fairness but once the judicial machinery is set in motion, the ex-president does not have the power to stop the proceedings: "no man is above the law." Only time will tell what legal consequences may ensue.

As for the insurrectionists, hundreds have been arrested. A large number of them have been tried and convicted; one received a sentence of forty-one months or roughly three and a half years. That individual, and others like him, will have plenty of time to reflect upon their criminal behavior on behalf of a narcissist who fooled them into believing a preposterous lie. Even the most fervent rioters may find their ardor cooling off after a prolonged stay in prison. Upon being incarcerated, I'm sure some of them will be asking themselves whether their actions on January 6 were worth months or even years of their lives confined behind bars and being branded a felon, which will affect their families and their future ability to earn a livelihood. How sad for those who come to their senses, to discover they were hoodwinked into committing desperate and unpatriotic crimes that landed them inside a prison, crimes based on Trump's Big Lie.

The prosecutors have started from the bottom up; some of the mildest charges supported by incontrovertible video evidence were presented during the first trials. The prosecutors are following the connections, lines of communication, and financial resources from one person to the next. Such an approach builds a stronger foundation for the coming trials of those rioters charged with the most serious felonies. Charges of seditious conspiracy have entered the courtroom; if convicted, the defendants will face lengthy prison sentences. Oath-keeper Joshua Hames has already pled guilty to *seditious conspiracy*. Numerous defendants have pled guilty to other charges; probably the light is beginning to dawn on them that they were being used as expendable pawns. In street parlance, they are doing another man's time for him.

Those jailed Trump supporters won't be able to do Trump's dirty work for a while; others may think twice before engaging in such reckless violence at his beck-and-call. By now some of them may even understand why the courts did not uphold any of Trump challenges. The judges did not see appropriate evidence to proceed because his lawyers had no evidence of voter fraud to present. It remains only for some of his arrested-and-convicted followers to realize that Trump, their Once-Great-Hero, has been deceiving them and playing them for chumps. At the very least, they should understand by now that such criminal riots will not be tolerated by the nation and will only lead to their arrest and prison sentence.

It is well understood that there are Trump loyalists who exhibit all the signs of zealous cult members but, thankfully, not all Trump supporters are as bad as the worst. A few of the rioters must be feeling the prick of conscience by now; they must realize that Trump misled them into believing a concocted lie and compounded his falsehoods by inciting them to commit crimes for which they, and not him, will have to answer. Even if they do not experience remorse or a moral awakening, for practical reasons alone they must see the serious legal trouble that awaits them when they cross the line from free speech to criminal behavior.

That's why, given the historic importance of January 6th's insurrectionary attack, Trump's other recent utterances seem less shocking, almost innocuous by comparison. His statement about how he would "consider" a pardon for rioters if they are convicted of crimes committed during the January 6 insurrection, is merely another link in the long chain of "I can do anything" promises he dangles before his base.

"Stick with me; I'll defend the rioters who tried to overthrow the government!"

Where reason fails, deception thrives.

****

The GOP and American Democracy (2021-22)

Like any "I'm always right" figure, the present GOP leader makes sure to keep close control over the beliefs and mood swings of his most ardent supporters. All too typical for Trump, there's no understanding of what happened on January 6 *in a long-term historical context.* He shows little or no remorse for the dangerous flames his words helped to fan; he stews in his own ego and cannot accept the fact that Americans voted him out of office.

His false claims and inflammatory remarks incited his most vociferous supporters to attempt to overturn the 2020 presidential election and yet he still can't figure out where the danger to American democracy arises: *it comes from him!* That they didn't succeed was no thanks to him. The news media and general population are now tracking with heightened curiosity every move and statement he makes, especially those comments reflecting a bias against democratic values. Certainly, if he has chosen to put personal ambition above all else, even above the obligations found in a president's most solemn oath to protect the nation and the Constitution, he deserves the closest public scrutiny.

Historically, American citizens have come to expect presidents to defend constitutional principles, not abuse or bend them for selfish purposes. An argument can be made that Trump broke the oath he took as president; there were numerous examples *before* January 6, 2021 to support such a notion but the catastrophic events of that day, more than any other, reveal a man psychologically unable to abide by majority rule following a presidential election. This is no mere error of judgment or uncontrolled burst of temper; the violent actions of that day involved careful pre-planning and coordination as well as the language of exhortation needed to ignite the necessary spark. Who but Trump could get a crowd of supporters so riled up that it was prepared to turn itself into a mob of violent insurrectionists intent on endangering the very soul of America?

Perhaps not everyone in the crowd participated in the invasion of the Capitol Building but a large mass of people did, enough to create a deadly war-like atmosphere all out of proportion to the right of peaceful assembly granted by the Constitution. In urging the crowd on, Trump incited them to riot and insurrection. He thus betrayed his oath to "preserve, protect and defend" the Constitution *before all other considerations.* The president not only enforces the laws of the land but he must obey them himself. Presidents should appreciate the historical, legal, and moral basis for America's constitutional philosophy and commitment to the rule of law. Instead, Trump shocked the world with what he tried to get away with when left to his own devices, free of the ethical and constitutional restraints acknowledged by previous presidents. He would destroy America's tradition of a peaceful transition of power from one president to the next in a futile effort to overturn a free and fair election.

To think: the House of Representatives has impeached him *twice* to counter his abuse of power and to slow down his "I can do anything!" conceit from wreaking even greater harm. At this critical juncture in American history, at this moment of national and global crisis brought on by the COVID-19 pandemic and its aftermath, where was Trump? If nothing else, where was his empathy? Did he ever ask: what can I do to help make things better? Did he wonder about how he could offer aid and sympathy to those bearing the brunt of the pandemic? Did he inquire what could be done to address the burgeoning economic crisis, with worse months yet to follow?

Even *after* he was voted out-of-office, what was the first thought that came to Trump's mind? Was it for the distress and struggles of Americans or was it for himself? An ex-president could easily have helped boost the spirits of Americans by making timely appearances in support of doctors and hospitals working to stop the spread of the Coronavirus. He could have promised a good faith effort to respect the next administration and support its efforts to curtail the pandemic and strengthen the economy. He could have congratulated the new president and wished him well! But for Trump, there would be none of that spirit of cooperation and compassion.

Instead, he would bring dozens of frivolous lawsuits, completely without merit, in a desperate but vain attempt *to overturn* the election. He ignored the protocol that an ex-president should graciously accept the fact that the American people, by voting, expressed their preference for a new president; his last task should be to complete the peaceful transfer of power from the outgoing to the incoming administration. Every president before him behaved in this respectful and civil manner. But not Trump! No, he had to act and speak in a way that did nothing less than touch off an insurrectionary riot in Washington D.C.

You would think such an event might have shocked him back to reality but apparently it was to his liking; as to the other expectations, they meant nothing to him. Now he has to act surprised about what happened and be ready to deny at the drop of a hat that he personally had anything to do with it. That's par for the course for Trump: to create a situation wherein his angry words prompt his loyal supporters to attack Congress and yet leave himself enough room to deny that he did or said anything that might indicate his complicity for the January 6th Riot. We have had four years of his denials and lies when he's cornered; the leopard can't change its spots . . . even in the last days of the presidency.

He, of all people, now calls "Foul!" He asserts "people are picking on him" or "the election was stolen" or "the media persecutes him" and so on. He puts on his happy-sad face and reassures his base that everything is going well for him. One gets the feeling that even if he were convicted of a crime and wound up in jail, he would still reassure his followers that everything was going well. He would try to convince them that his legal troubles were happening according to plan; he would tell them that he must take a short break from the political circuit in order to appear in court or to serve his time in prison . . . but keep sending in those contributions, they help pay his lawyers' fees! Thus always, when ambition outstrips conscience.

Sometimes it helps to look down the road to try and see what developments the future might bring. Now, after a rather long silence and staying mostly out of sight, the ex-president thought of something new to say; he announced that he'll look for a way *to pardon the insurrectionists* currently being put on trial. That's part of his personality; he caved in to his desperate desire to let his base know that he, the omnipotent Donald J. Trump, will be able to protect them, come what may, if they are arrested and convicted of crimes, even serious felonies. What better sure-fire way to do that than that to appeal to his most ardent loyalists: those excitable men and women who are the quickest to go off the deep end and the first to engage in reckless acts of violence against his enemies?

Three years from now, if he gets re-elected, he promises his base he will consider "pardons" for the insurrectionists even though top U.S. law enforcement officials consider them domestic terrorists. One wonders if that could be Trump's new slogan: "Elect me and I'll pardon the insurrectionists! I'll pardon the men and women who committed felonies while rioting, destroying property, and threatening the lives of policemen and members of Congress in order to stop the certification of a free election held by secret ballot: vote for ME and I'll let those rioters go FREE!"

If this becomes the first slogan or promise of Trump's 2024 campaign, as well it might, I must confess I'm not all that worried about how this might help or hurt his chance of success: his mouth is always going to get him in more trouble, not less. If we thought the first four years of Trumpism felt like a circus, a surreal corruption of time-honored norms and traditions, we must remember all that occurred while Trump was still relatively healthy and robust. Now he slumps on stage like he would fall if the podium weren't there to hold him; his mood appears to be a curious blending of anger, sadness, and personal resentment against a long list of enemies.

For many Americans, it doesn't matter whether he's described as crazy or sane, clever or dumb, crafty or demented; what they know is that he poses a threat to American democracy. I suppose that's why some of us had trouble responding to this latest half-baked statement of Trump's; there was a brief shock before the dust settled. The news media dutifully noted it before moving on to cover more pressing issues. Even Trump's expertise in garnering publicity seems to be growing weak and ineffective; the "shock" value he routinely exploited to upset the apple cart has diminished considerably over the last few years.

There was hardly time to raise an eyebrow; his statement he might pardon the rioters was low down on the Richter scale. It's just more Trumpism. He's made so many dubious pronouncements over the last few years that this latest "epiphany" of his just seemed like one more absurdity: another demonstration of his warped imagination and questionable judgment for future historians to record. Naturally, it is a serious matter that he might try again to bend and warp the Constitution to do his bidding, but there are various safeguards built into the three branches of government model that will not yield to his strange notions of the presidency. His legal troubles would seem to indicate that he cannot overcome the nation's commitment to the Constitution, including no man above the law.

In any event, such a remark is only the tip of the iceberg; the greater danger resides in the submerged parts that we cannot yet see wherein the Far Right pursues policies and actions injurious to the democratic nature of the nation. Even so, the average American must sometimes wonder: what goes through Trump's mind when his Ego lights up? I believe Trump must mull things over in a uniquely narcissistic fashion. His thinking probably goes something like this:

"I am pledged by oath to defend and protect the Constitution and America. Despite that pledge, I chose to ignite my loyalists into attacking Congress in the Capitol Building in order to reverse an election I clearly lost ('Oh, I can't admit it, I can't!') If I am president I will exercise my presidential powers to issue pardons for these rioters of whatever they may be convicted: whether guilty of criminal trespass, vandalism, destruction of property, obstruction of justice, bodily assault on police officers, seditious conspiracy or attempting to find and hang Nancy Pelosi and Mike Pence. Whether we call it mayhem and mêlée or riot and insurrection, doesn't matter to me. I will override those lawful verdicts, whenever they occur, reached by a fair-minded impaneled jury in an American courtroom!" His reasoning continues:

"I will issue pardons not based on exceptional circumstances or call for medical compassion but on my own personal indulgence. I will consider doing this even though I know such pardons are not reflective of the highest moral and legal standards of the country. I can pardon a crony in crime because that's the way The Donald rolls. Sure, I will be abusing the power of the presidency because I figured out that I can get away with it due to a loophole in the Constitution; the Founding Fathers never envisioned a Narcissist like me! I will pardon those *guilty* of insurrection even though it goes against the Constitution and the courts and the will of the people: I say to hell with them. I will do it!"

114

What kind of all-time rock-bottom nadir in political ethics would that be? That would be a new kind of American madness, far exceeding anything the nation has experienced previously, even from the most nutty and extremist wing of the GOP. And yet that's the kind of assessment we may ascribe to Trump's situation; first, we witnessed his involvement with the violent riot of January 6th and, second, his not-so-subtle hint of a pledge *to pardon the perpetrators!* We witnessed his mental and emotional inability to cope with his election loss; we watched him fall down the rabbit hole when he failed to issue a timely and powerful condemnation of the insurrection.

The president, pledged to defend against insurrection, did nothing hour after hour during that riotous afternoon. Who has become the enemy of America's constitutional democracy if not Trump? He has not grown a conscience or a sense of shame since last we saw him in the White House. There's no admission he lost the election; there's no condemnation of the rioters. There's no recognition of the calamitous and unprecedented dangers posed to our democracy by riotous Trump loyalists behaving like a lynch mob. There's no recognition that it was *his remarks* that served as one of the sparks of the insurrection, and most likely the primary one.

He cannot speak honestly and frankly to the issue so he must hem and haw, misdirect and act the fool when nothing else in his bag of tricks can save him. There's only one suggestion he managed to offer when referencing the attack upon Congress; *he will pardon violent men and women convicted of riot and insurrection*! Does he think he is laying the cornerstone of a new country to be ruled by him? Does he think that such a scheme will distract the American people from remembering and judging the January 6th insurrection?

If I worry at all, I'm fearful that Trump might travel to Russia and move in with Putin in the Kremlin! Then America would have not one but two formidable enemies with whom to contend. If they decided to work together, that would double their power. It is unlikely to happen, thankfully, but if one were given the choice of having to fight one of these two men, both holed up in Moscow, who would you fear more? Tough call, isn't it? Putin is strong but no one knows better than Trump how to divide a nation and besmirch America's multicultural heritage.

Trump says if he is elected....What will his next gem be? Well, the gamblers are gathering, making bets and giving odds. They do so while keeping in mind that Trump's narcissistic instability may become so blatant over the coming months that not everyone in the Republican Party will wish to defend him or recycle him as their nominee. Indeed, the GOP may yet split over Trump, his values, and his "Me First" attitude. In any and all situations where he gets to decide policy, that selfish streak is always going to be the primary factor in his decision-making; he is risking the largest ego implosion of any political leader in American history, one who is sure to leave a terrible and permanent stain as part of his legacy, such as it is.

He has caused the entire nation incredibly difficult moments. He appears to be in bed with the wealthiest families, corporations, and campaign donors (meant figuratively). In truth, he is the most arrogant president in our history; at times he appears completely ignorant of our bedrock constitutional principles or willfully disdainful and oblivious to them. Ask yourself: how many times have you heard Trump discuss the philosophical values and constitutional principles upon which our nation stands?

Perhaps his grandfather who came from Germany (not Sweden) would understand the need to act like an autocrat. After all, the princes of Germany were very nearly absolute rulers in their own little fiefdoms. Trump would like to think of America as his own fiefdom if he could, for that would make the country "easier" to rule. Perhaps if he becomes president again he could pass an edict that Democrats are to be excluded from all election cycles and only Republicans will be allowed to run for office and vote. The U.S. under Trump could become a one-party state under the aegis of the GOP. Wouldn't that make him deliriously happy!

The Germanic gene for an authoritarian personality never quite seems to disappear in the Trump clan, does it? Three generations in America was simply not enough time to teach Grandpa, Dad, and Donald how to read and appreciate the Constitution. This most notorious scion of the Trump male lineage, a man who appears to enjoy suffocating civil manners under the weight of his narcissism, is the worst of the bunch. He doesn't read and he doesn't care that he doesn't read; he only acknowledges democratic institutions when they get in his way. He shows a growing belligerence whenever he is forced to submit to laws by forces stronger than he can handle, such as Congress, the courts, or the people themselves. Perhaps another political position for him (besides "I'll pardon the rioters!") would go something like this:

"I will give myself the power to suspend the Constitution whenever I choose if any of its provisions get in my way and prevent me (along with my wealthy backers) from controlling the nation's financial policies to our advantage, unimpeded by Democrats." Oh shucks, that's much too long for a bumper strip, isn't it? It should be shorter, like "I'm here to help the rich!" His loyalists will get the message: "If I get impeached a third time, my followers know what to do; they will make the insurrection of January 6th look like a Boy Scout picnic."

That's where we entered this historical circle, this circus, this travesty of a play with fair-minded Americans forced to watch Trump continuously make a fool or tyrant out of himself. His charismatic cultism appears to be running out of fuel; he will need to spend enormous amounts of money and time fighting the multiple indictments coming his way. If the GOP sticks with him, an indicted defendant facing ninety-one felony charges, as their standard-bearer; if they stick

118

with him even after he is convicted of multiple felonies, then the GOP will only have itself to blame for the condemnation they earn nationally and internationally. Their choices will be excoriated by historians in the sharpest language imaginable for years to come.

So, in the final analysis, should we be particularly upset by Trump's unwise comments that he might pardon the violent insurrectionists who tried to disrupt our democratic government? Not much. After all, it is only logical to expect more of the same in the coming days and weeks. He cannot stop his own mouth from uttering illogical and anti-democratic sentiments; today's unbelievable "shocker" will simply be followed by another one tomorrow or next week. He seems to learn so little from his past mistakes, including his inability to recognize them, let alone take responsibility for them. So why does the GOP tolerate or promote him as their spokesman?

He knows how to play to the Far Right crowd, how to control and stir their emotions and manipulate their beliefs and actions. January 6 made that point abundantly clear. After he lost the election, all he could think about was starting the "Big Lie" Campaign. In doing so, he inspired his followers to behave violently in a futile effort to prevent Congress from carrying out its lawful duties. And now all he can think to say is that he *might* pardon these same men and women who perpetrated these crimes of riot and mayhem! If that came to pass, it likely would lead to Impeachment #3: what is it that they say? "The third time's the charm!"

American history is moving a little too fast to waste time on such idiotic and immoral behavior keeping company with antiquated and authoritarian braggadocio. Our society is changing rapidly, as it has done numerous times before, and no doubt will do so again in the future. Major popular movements are developing around crucial issues and even existential crises, such as protecting the environment and taking decisive action to slow global warming. People are pushing for change based on reason and science and their momentum cannot be stopped.

The GOP can bring in their poster boy for Narcissism if they wish; they can even try to promote a false mythology about him but he won't be able to stop the groups coalescing into a fighting opposition. He can be the champion of the Status Quo, buttressed by a not-so-subtle movement of white supremacy aimed at negating racial progress in America. He can try to undo what millions of Americans have achieved and willed as their legacy to the future, but he will not succeed.

We know Trump and his cronies do the bidding of the coal, oil, and gas big-wigs but time is running out for them, due to the growing dangers posed by climate change which will outweigh all the posturing of the hypocrites and reactionaries. The Trumpistas are merely fighting to protect their power and wealth, not to build a strong or fairer America. They are struggling to preserve the status quo and "stop time;" the most reactionary among them would turn back the hands on the clock if they could. But time doesn't go backwards and popular movements, along with technological advances, must always keep moving forward.

As an example: in the news recently, Biden kept the promise he made to appoint the first black woman to the Supreme Court. The president engaged in the search for the best female black lawyer or judge to nominate to the Supreme Court: a historic first and another sign of hope for the future. That's a small but promising development that is both positive and inspiring![21] Granted, the court has been captured by a conservative majority but that will not last forever.

All the Justices are, in the final analysis, limited by what the Constitution allows and prohibits. In time, the wisdom of the Founding Fathers will triumph over even the most conservative Justices. Meanwhile, millions of Americans are on the move and Congress must try to keep pace with the changing times. Taking the long view, Americans should focus on the nation living up to its reputation for equality of opportunity and reward, regardless of race, ethnicity, gender, or place of national origin.

The real America is not to be subverted or destroyed by the rightwing of the Republican Party, however frightful its influence sometimes appears to be. Neither Trump nor the GOP can stop such movements or stay these popular forces pushing for substantive social change whose time has come. Rightwing

---

[21] Ketanji Brown Jackson was confirmed by the U.S. Senate on April 7, 2022.

Republicans may try to delay or prevent changes now underway but in the end they will be swept aside. We must not get sucked into the negativity of cynicism that Trump brings to everything he touches. Currently, he is an out-of-office, twice-impeached ex-president soon to be facing multiple felony charges. Morally speaking, how much lower than that can a man or a party sink?

If Trump Republicans are opposed to everything the Democrats favor, then what policies can the Republican Party put forward independently in dealing with society's needs and crises? Ultimately, they must either put up or shut up; if they cannot deliver answers for climate change, homelessness, housing shortages, protection of Social Security, elimination of mass shootings and other major social problems, they cannot move the country forward. They cannot improve the commitment of the Constitution's Preamble to "insure domestic Tranquility" and "promote the general Welfare." Certainly, economic cycles can prove problematic and new crises are likely to occur; the GOP leaders cannot deal effectively with them by staying put, by defending the Status Quo, by opposing progressive measures and by refusing to take action other than to block Democratic initiatives.

They cannot achieve much of anything by not cooperating with the Democrats in Congress. They cannot help move the country forward in a bipartisan manner by bringing to the foreground a pompous narcissist who knows little of the ideals of American democracy; he appears to know nothing of the courageous defenders of liberty who fought to establish our new nation based on popular sovereignty, even though such brave men and women are found on every page of America's story. The American people simply are seeking a better life; as a civil rights song once reminded protestors risking their lives for justice:

We've been 'buked and we've been scorned,
We've been talked about sure sure born,
But we'll never turn back
Until we're all living free
And we have equality.

It is the great mistake of all conservative, reactionary, and fascist parties to think they can stop humanity's march toward freedom and justice. The Republican Party doesn't appear to seek social change or redress that benefits anyone but themselves. No doubt it is why the GOP leaders have had to resort to such questionable and unethical tactics in the first place, as we have seen in recent years. They prefer to practice hypocrisy and deceit; they prefer to engage in gerrymandering to redraw districts to clump Republican areas together, no matter how oddly shaped and unwarranted that district is compared to any social metric *other than race*, rather than allow direct, honest, and universal voting determine the election's outcome.

They promote "voter reform" (i.e., voter suppression) laws because they are acutely aware that they have not been winning the majority vote in presidential elections and have not done so but once since 1988: thirty-two years.[22]   Rather than accept and defend majority electoral democracy in action, they have decided like thieves-in-the-night to abandon their faith in the American election system when it suits their purpose; they have chosen to spread the Big Lie and have gone so far as to attempt to subvert a presidential election through a violent insurrection.

The GOP game plan is obvious: win elections by outspending the Democratic Party with dark money and by paying for a series of "hit job" political ads. They also have adopted the propaganda strategy of "The bigger the lie..." and hope to gain ground by the repetition of false and scurrilous accusations: most no better than slimy character assassination, the kind of lies normally associated with conscienceless scoundrels hiding amid the dregs of society.

Because their falsehoods and misleading statements may still not be enough, they have also focused on tilting elections in their favor by passing voter suppression laws and by putting Trump loyalists in key positions to oversee election results. If all these strategies combined are not enough, the GOP leaders may choose "to look the other way" if Trump leads the Far Right in a second attempt to overthrow the government. The GOP is becoming less and less a reputable political party and more and more a collection of rich individuals seeking to maintain their own privilege at the expense of everyone else. The current

---

[22] The Republican candidate won the Electoral College in 2000 and 2016 but not the popular vote.

GOP leaders and Trump loyalists have become the very enemy against which Republicans of an earlier generation *warned us*. The party's current leaders certainly appear to condone domestic terrorism when they fail to condemn the violent insurrectionists of January 6, 2021 in no uncertain terms.

Their silence becomes acquiescence. And that's all Trump's influence, is it not? The GOP leaders and common-man Republicans must now decide if they still wish to follow Trump wherever he goes, even if he leads them into the fires of hell or over the edge of a cliff. They are like hypnotized lemmings following a narcissist who is bereft of a moral lodestar. The Republicans are nothing if not flexible with their variety of vote-stealing and vote-nullifying techniques; unfortunately, they cannot speak for a true majority of Americans. In truth, their extremist elements barely remain within the American political forum at all: that's another well-known step for any budding authoritarian figure and the loyalist pack of wolves he leads.

It is not just Trump who needs watching; it is the whole damn Republican Party!

****

Made in the USA
Columbia, SC
09 November 2024

45788689R00070